Crazy & Obsessed
Addicted to Relationships

Crazy & Obsessed
Addicted to Relationships

Crazy & Obsessed
Addicted to Relationships

Crazy & Obsessed
Addicted to Relationships
A Crazy & Obsessed Series (Book 1)

Crazy & Obsessed
Addicted to Relationships

Crazy & Obsessed
Addicted to Relationships

Crazy & Obsessed
Addicted to Relationships
A Crazy & Obsessed Series (Book 1)

© 2019

Crazy & Obsessed
Addicted to Relationships

All rights reserved. No part of this publication may be reproduced, distributed, or transmitted in any form or by any means, including photocopying, recording, or other electronic or mechanical methods, without the prior written permission of the publisher, except in the case of brief quotations embodied in critical reviews and certain other noncommercial uses permitted by copyright law.

Cover Design by Lara Wynter @Wynter Designs

Crazy & Obsessed
Addicted to Relationships

Table of Contents

Foreword
13

Prologue
My Tragic Love Life
15

Chapter One
I Am Not Crazy
25

Chapter Two
What Is Wrong With Us?
33

Chapter Three
If Relationships Are Forced, They Are Not Based On Love
41

Chapter Four
Time To Let Go
46

Crazy & Obsessed
Addicted to Relationships

Chapter Five
We Are All Affected
58

Chapter Six
Society Dooms Us All
68

Chapter Seven
We Never Get Over It
71

Chapter Eight
Identity Crisis
75

Chapter Nine
Innocent Abusers
80

Chapter Ten
The Demise Of XY
86

Chapter Eleven
Happy Wife, Happy Life
88

Crazy & Obsessed
Addicted to Relationships

Chapter Twelve
Mutual Breakups Are A Hoax
93

Chapter Thirteen
The Broken Heart
95

Chapter Fourteen
Get Over It Already
99

Chapter Fifteen
You Are Crazy. Deal With It!
104

Chapter Sixteen
Who The Hell Are You?!
107

Chapter Seventeen
Stranger Danger
112

Chapter Eighteen
Societal Rules Shall Die
117

Crazy & Obsessed
Addicted to Relationships

Chapter Nineteen
Seriously, We Do Not Know What The Fuck We Want
124

Chapter Twenty
Taking Our Lives Back
135

Chapter Twenty-One
We Can Heal
140

Chapter Twenty-Two
My Obsession
146

Chapter Twenty-Three
Stop Judging Us Based On Our Pasts!
162

Chapter Twenty-Four
Are We Just Not Good Enough?
169

Chapter Twenty-Five
We Are All Closet Sociopaths
184

Crazy & Obsessed
Addicted to Relationships

Chapter Twenty-Six
Pick Yourself Up!
188

Chapter Twenty-Seven
The Face Behind The Mask
194

Chapter Twenty-Eight
Blind Love
198

Chapter Twenty-Nine
What Is Jealousy?
201

Chapter Thirty
We Are Selfish Assholes
206

Chapter Thirty-One
All Work, No Play
220

Chapter Thirty-Two
Learning To Love
230

Crazy & Obsessed
Addicted to Relationships

Chapter Thirty-Three
Be Real
240

Epilogue
The Turn Around
255

Conclusion
We Are Over. Right?
262

Foreword

The purpose of my personal love story is, not to advocate for out-of-the-ordinary, abnormal, self-destructive, and, sometimes, abusive, behaviors, but to provide insight into how and why people engage in these behaviors.

I believe there are still standards to be upheld when it comes to engaging in a relationship with another person, and that there will always be consequences when certain behaviors go awry, so I am, by no means, advocating for any of the actions that people engage in.

The purpose of my story is two-fold:

Crazy & Obsessed
Addicted to Relationships

To help people see that they are not alone in the actions they partake in when they are heartbroken and in pain, and,

To minimize the stigma of pain as something to be ashamed of, and to allow people to recognize that the actions they make when they are in pain are due to sporadic and uncontrollable emotions, not personalities, and should not be used to define them as people.

We need to take a stand against having to feel "normal" and "sane" after a traumatic experience, such as the loss of someone we loved and trusted. We need to speak out against shaming people when they are only acting out of natural instincts.

It is easy for us to point blame and criticize when we are not the ones deep in the throes of those emotions, but we also need to realize that everyone eventually falls victim to feelings.

Here is my story.

Prologue

My Tragic Love Life

Me: "I love you so much, and I will never leave your side. These rings will stay on both your finger and mine until the end of time because I've known, from the first day I met you, that I want to marry you."

Him: "I love you too! I'm so glad you're in my life, and I promise to love you and grow old with you until the day I die."

The next afternoon

Crazy & Obsessed
Addicted to Relationships

Him (via text): "We're done."

Me (dumbfounded): "Wait. What!?"

Him (frustrated and annoyed): "I said we're over. We. Are. Done. Do NOT message me or talk to me anymore. We are done."

Me: "Wait, what the fuck is going on?! What the hell changed since last night?! Talk to me about what's going on!"

Silence

Me: "Are you there?!??"

Silence

Me: "Fucking answer me! You can't ignore me like this!"

Silence

Me: "Talk to me!! What the hell happened!? You promised to marry me, and now you're dumping me!??! We've been together for six fucking years!!"

Silence

Me (thinking): Maybe he's working or too busy to realize that I'm texting him. I should call him. That'll get him to talk to me.

Calls

Voicemail

Crazy & Obsessed
Addicted to Relationships

Calls again

Voicemail

Calls ten more times

Voicemail

Me (via text): "Please pick up your fucking phone!"

No answer

Me (via text): "Please pick up your phone and talk to me about this! I love you so much!"

Silence

Me: "Can I come over, and we can talk about this?"

Silence

Me (tears running down my face): "I can fake sick and leave work right now, and we can talk!"

Silence

Me: "If you don't pick up, I am going to mix a bottle of vodka with a shit ton of Tylenol tonight. PAY ATTENTION TO ME!!"

Silence

Me (thinking, heart pounding rapidly): This can't be happening. What the hell did I do? Is he seeing someone else? Did I say something wrong last night? Were any parts of our relationship real? What the fuck is going on? What the FUCK is going on?! Did I just threaten to kill myself? That was messed up. He knows I'm just messing around anyway, right? Not like he fucking cares what happens to me. He's probably not even reading any of this. He FUCKING BLOCKED me, didn't he? Fuck it. I'm going to go cry myself to sleep. I hate my life! I hate my STUPID LIFE!

Later that day back at the apartment, the police show up.

Police: "Excuse me, miss. You're going to have to come with us. We have reason to believe that you are a danger to yourself and possibly others."

Me (feigning ignorance and faking a smile): "What!? I'm fine! I have no idea what you're talking about. See, perfectly happy and normal!"

Police: "Come with us, miss."

Me: "Why? There is nothing wrong with me. I just got back from work. I don't have thoughts about harming myself or others. I don't know where you're getting this information from!"

Police: "We received an anonymous call informing us that you are going to hurt yourself tonight, and we need to bring you into the hospital to keep you safe."

Me: "What the fuck!? Who the fuck called you?"

Police: "Miss, please come with us. Please don't make us utilize physical force."

Crazy & Obsessed
Addicted to Relationships

Me: "God fucking damn it. FINE!!"

Inside the lobby of a psychiatric institute, after three hours of waiting and four hours of nonstop interrogation...

Nurse: "Excuse me, miss. We have evidence to believe that you are a danger to yourself. Someone sent over text messages that you had plans of harming yourself with a bottle of vodka and some Tylenol pills tonight. You need to voluntarily sign yourself in for a 72-hour minimum treatment by order of the law and your job. You are not allowed to return to work until we can successfully determine that you are no longer a danger to yourself. If you do not consent, we will be held liable for your safety, and we will be forced to take you to court on accounts of mental insanity. We will need to hold possession of your belongings: phone, keys, wallet, and any other objects except for the clothing on your back. Please sit tight in this solitary room until we can find you a bed upstairs."

Me (thinking): That fucking asshole! First, he proposes to me. Then, he breaks up with me through text and ignores my 350 messages. Now, he throws me into a FUCKING LOONY BIN!?!! FUCKING SOCIOPATH!! Who the hell does he think he is!?! I'm a person! Not a fucking doll!!! I FUCKING HATE HIM!! I love him, but I HATE HIM!!!

Me (angry, in tears, and shouting): "I'm not crazy! I'm just hurt and pissed off! And how the fuck am I supposed to hurt myself with money!? Really!?"

Silence

Quiet

Darkness

Emptiness

Loneliness

Silence

Sixteen hours later...

Nurse: "Alright, miss. Come with us. We need to have you examined by a psychotherapist before we can assign you to your room."

Me: "Can you please stop calling me "miss"? I have a name. It's on that board you won't take your eyes off of."

Silence

Me (annoyed): "Really? Okay, MISS, you have me on lockdown with 24/7 supervision. What am I supposed to do, NOT BREATHE TO DEATH?"

Nurse: "Miss, please behave, or I will be forced to have you restrained."

Me: "I'm not even doing anyt..."

Nurse: "I said, BEHAVE!"

Restrained and in the therapist's office (or rather, a dark and empty crapshack conference room)...

Crazy & Obsessed
Addicted to Relationships

Psychotherapist: "So, how are you feeling right now?"

Me: "Why do you guys always ask that as a starter question?"

Psychotherapist: "We find that patients tend to respond better to questions and statements that show we care."

Me: "Do you really care though? Or are you just following a script so you can go home after your shift?"

Psychotherapist: "So, how are you feeling right now?"

Me: "You totally dodged my question! What happened to, "showing that we care"?!"

Psychotherapist: "Please just answer the question."

Me: "For fuck's sake. Fine, I feel like crap. Are you fucking happy now!?"

Psychotherapist: "I am always happy, and you can be too. Also, crap is not a feeling."

Me (chuckling): "Wait, wait. You're ALWAYS happy??! I call bullshit, mainly because you totally have resting bitch face right now."

Psychotherapist: "Please watch your language. I am here to help you because I understand what you are going through, and I want to help you get out of here as soon as possible. Now, please, tell me how you are feeling."

Me: "You don't give a shit about me! If you do, you would focus on what I'm saying and my tone of voice rather than focusing on writing, whatever the hell you're writing, on that clipboard! Also, watch my language?!?!? Does it fucking look like we're in church?!? Oh no, save me, Jesus! I can't wait to get out of here so I can cut myself with A DOLLAR BILL!"

Security guard (holding my arms down): "PLEASE STOP RESISTING AND COMPLY!"

Me: "Damn, dude. Chill the fuck out. Fine, I'll fucking behave."

Psychotherapist: "Let's try this one more time. How are you feeling right now?"

Me: "Like crap."

Psychotherapist: "Like I said, crap is not a feeling."

Me: "Okay. Like pissed-off crap."

Psychotherapist: "Why are you pissed off?"

Me: "Wouldn't you be pissed off if your son-of-a-bitch fiancé broke up with you for no reason and with no explanation, through FUCKING TEXT of all things, after promising to love you forever, ignores you all day, and then gets you locked up in the loony bin without answering your 60 phone calls? We were together for SIX FUCKING YEARS! He didn't think I deserved a little more respect than silence after being together for six years?!"

Psychotherapist: "Okay, and how does that make you feel?"

Crazy & Obsessed
Addicted to Relationships

Me: "Really, bitch? You asked that already. LIKE PISSED-OFF CRAP!!!"

Psychotherapist: "I am afraid you will have to stay here for a few days. You seem very hostile, and I fear that you will harm yourself or someone else, particularly your fiancé, if I let you leave here tonight untreated."

Me (thinking): Wait, hold the fucking phone. Back up about a mile here. First, what the fuck do you mean by "untreated"? What kind of fucking treatment are you planning on doing to me!? You better not overdose me with a shit ton of pills, that you don't even know works or not, and then use that as an excuse to keep me in here longer! Second, you asked the same question twice, both times which I answered, and suddenly I'm the crazy one? Third, since when does feeling angry because of a terrible situation equate to being suicidal and homicidal? I can't express my emotions without being deemed a psychotic murderer? Were you even listening to anything I said, or were you deliberately trying to piss me off on purpose so you can use that as an excuse to keep me here!? What the fuck is wrong with you people!? I am a fucking human being, not some doll that you can throw around from place to place just because I'm currently a little erratic!

Psychotherapist: "Are you okay? You haven't said anything in a while."

Me (thinking): It was ten seconds, bitch. Get off my back. Besides, the more I say, the more you can use what I say against me to fucking LOCK ME UP EVEN LONGER!

Me (mumbling): "Yeah. I'm okay."

Psychotherapist: "Alright then. Let me show you to your room."

Me: "Can I just make one phone call? It's important! Just one!"

Psychotherapist: "I'm sorry, miss. It's after hours. The other residents need to sleep. You can use the phone tomorrow."

Me: "I'M NOT FUCKING CRAZY AND STOP CALLING ME "MISS"!!"

The doors close.

I remain alone.

In a dark, damp room.

Locked up.

In solitary confinement.

Chapter One

I Am Not Crazy

"To be crazy is to possess the mindset of craziness. Only by acknowledging that the acts we create are flawed, will they be flawed." ℒ

I am sure I am not the only one who has been through crazy and psychotic messes after a terrible breakup, a breakup that feels like betrayal, from someone I once loved deeply and thought returned the same feelings. It is completely natural to feel like we are going insane when we fall from the very top of the positive emotions' spectrum to the very bottom.

Crazy & Obsessed
Addicted to Relationships

You probably thought, or still think, that you are crazy for becoming obsessive over someone you love who will not love you back, and there is good reason for that because, for so long, everyone around you has told you that certain types of behavior either resemble that of a stalker or that of a serial killer.

But just because we act out in response to the pain we feel, does not make us psychotic or evil. If these actions persisted for months and months, then that is a different story, but feeling hurt does not have to equate to being ashamed of the way we feel in response to traumatic situations.

We want to love so badly that, when we are let down or when we are betrayed, we revert to childlike states and act out impulsively and wildly as a coping mechanism.

We have been given one knowledge of information for so long, to meet someone, fall in love, and get married, that when that suddenly changes, we become confused and lost in our ways, unsure of which actions to engage in next.

We lose our conscience and our logic because the person we have fallen in love with and trusted has betrayed us, putting a dent in our knowledge of information without the option of another path.

What my synopsis above did not cover was, my 6-year relationship was not always full of love, promises, and fancy rings. About five months into the dating phase, my now ex-fiancé cheated on me. Inexperienced with long-term relationships at the time, my emotions started

Crazy & Obsessed
Addicted to Relationships

fucking around with me, telling me both to leave and to stay, to find someone new and to try to make it work.
But he was a charmer, and he was manipulative. He fed me lies and bullshit excuses of how he thought I was his soulmate and the other woman was just a mistake. He sucked me back in, and I became entrapped for the next six years.

Looking back now, it was obvious that he did not love me, or at least not enough to remain loyal. The cheating did not stop; it just became sneakier, and soon after, he stopped trying to hide it altogether. Woman after woman, bra after bra, excuse after excuse, but I still could not get out. It felt like I could not see the reality of what was going on.

I thought the cheating meant that I had to prove that I was good enough to be with him, like it was some sort of competition. I hated myself because he enjoyed being with other women more than he enjoyed being with me. I gave him everything I could to try to get him to stop cheating, including buying him everything he wanted, paying for his car, and paying rent I could not afford alone when he stopped working for five years. I had become his slave and caretaker, but he still did not stop.

Then the abuse came, first mental, then physical, and eventually, both simultaneously. I was called "bitch," "idiot," "stupid," "whore," "cunt," and everything in between. When I tried to defend myself, I was beat, first purely out of rage, and then daily. I went to work several times with a black eye, and I hid my bruises from my family. I told everyone around me that my relationship was amazing, and I could not be more in love.

Crazy & Obsessed
Addicted to Relationships

But inside, I was dying. I wanted out, but at the same time, I felt guilty for leaving after having invested so much time and energy into the toxic relationship. There had been a few times, 298 to be exact, where he had broken up with me, giving me the out that I wanted, but I did not take it. Instead, I chased him and begged for him to come back, making impossible promises I could not uphold, and losing more and more of myself each time.

Soon, I was trapped in an infinite loop where it felt almost instinctual to chase after him whenever he leaves, even when I consciously knew I should not. I started to feel like I was doing something wrong, with anxiety kicking in when I WAS NOT begging for him to come back.

Pretty fucked up, right?

But, like all addictions, love included, realization usually does not set in until AFTER hitting ROCK-BOTTOM. Being locked up in a psychiatric institute for six weeks, yes, six weeks! (the 72-hour voluntary stay they make you sign is a bullshit excuse for them to get you through the doors), was my rock-bottom.

Maybe I just needed space away from him to realize that I did not need him.

Maybe I needed an external physical force to keep me away from him and snap me out of my behaviors.

Maybe I just needed time alone to reminisce on all the pain that I had endured when I was with him.

Maybe part of me will always love him and want to be with him.

Crazy & Obsessed
Addicted to Relationships

Who knows?

I just know that I am out, and I do not want to go back in.

Why did I continue to stay in my toxic relationship after the FIRST time he cheated on me, or even after the second? Why do a lot of people continue to stay in terrible and abusive relationships?

Because of a little thing called "false hope."

When we enter new relationships, we become so infatuated by the charm of other people, seeing only the positive and putting them on pedestals. So, when they make the switch and begin to show their true colors, despite how malicious, we still try to reason with ourselves that they are just having an off-day, and that things will go back to normal if we have a little patience and wait around for them to recuperate.

The problem is, nobody has an off-day for six years straight! I did not know then what my tiny brain knows now. Maybe it was loneliness, maybe it was desperation, or maybe it was a combination of both, but I forced myself to hold on regardless of how much I was hurting.

I forced myself to continue loving a manipulative and abusive cheater. I believed that if I fought through the physical abuse and the infidelity, then maybe, FINALLY, I would have proven my love to him.

I realize the shit I have been through are not normal behaviors in relationships. But what I have learned is that, as messed up as the actions I engaged in were, those actions are much more common than we like to believe.

Crazy behaviors are what we tend to hide from the world to show others that nothing is wrong, or could ever be wrong, with us. Another moral I have learned is that, this whole time, I was fighting a battle with myself, not my ex, during and after the relationship.

The biggest demon I was facing was my emotions, and the more I tried to fight it, the more I lost. Part of me knew that calling out suicidal threats and staying with a man who beat me were out-of-the-ordinary behaviors.

However, I felt so hurt, alone, and sad that crying for help and staying in the comforting behaviors I have been so used to seemed to be the only ways, at the time, to relieve myself from those burdening emotions. I hated dealing with how I was feeling.

Emotions can pull us toward the highest highs and the lowest lows, and I just wanted them to disappear completely. We try so hard to keep ourselves together, blocking out all unpleasant emotions, that we leave ourselves feeling numb.

We would rather experience apathy and emptiness than experience pain, because pain means pain while apathy and emptiness mean lack of pain. Unfortunately, because I tried to numb myself, I also felt alone for years, unable to see past the darkness that I was consumed in, unable to escape the shit-hole life I was living in, and isolating myself from everyone I cared about. My biggest enemy was myself, and I could not see past the paradigm of loving someone I hated and hating someone I was supposed to love.

The crazy acts that I engaged in during my relationships and my breakups, the crazy acts we all engage in during our relationships and our breakups, come from a place of love and care rather than a place of insanity and psychosis. We expend so much energy and effort on someone, or something, because we cannot imagine what it would feel like to not have that person, or that thing, in our lives anymore.

Being emotional DOES NOT mean being a PSYCHOPATH. We deal with so many emotions at once that we become unsure of whether to give up or to persist, to accept or deny, to live or let live. When we are in relationships where we do not allow pain to affect us, we become numb to love, making it more difficult to give love back to ourselves.
Let me be the one to drill this into your head! You are NOT crazy!

We are NOT crazy!

Emotions can destroy the best of us and drive even the most level-headed person up the wall! It does NOT mean that we deserve to be sent to mental institutions; it means that we are experiencing feelings that are too overwhelming for us to handle in our current states of mind.

These feelings can be old or new; it DOES NOT MATTER. When the heart breaks, it breaks, and it takes the rest of the body down with it.

Crazy & Obsessed
Addicted to Relationships

Embrace that we are emotional creatures. The more we try to hide that we have feelings, the longer it takes for us to heal. Each relationship and each breakup did not teach me something about that specific person and what I should and should not be looking for in a partner.

Instead, each experience taught me something about myself and how I experience and handle emotions. Unless these emotions are suicidal or homicidal, why not just let them roam free?

Chapter Two

What Is Wrong With Us?

"We have become so hated by society that we even begin to hate ourselves. Our obedience is our Achilles' heel." ℒ

Love.

Dating.

Soulmates.

Promises.

Crazy & Obsessed
Addicted to Relationships

What do these words all have in common?

The first words that come to mind are "false beliefs." We all want that special someone to share our lives with, to share the good times and the bad, to have that shoulder to cry on, and to have hands to hold when we feel joyful.

We have longed for these moments from when we first experienced affection toward someone, whether it was our first crush in elementary school or our first kiss in high school. We reveled in being able to love someone, but with that naivety, our hearts were also shattered when those relationships ended.

Maybe some of you are the lucky ones who marry the first person you felt a connection with. The rest of us know, all too well, how it feels to open our hearts and our lives to one single person, to put so much power into the hands of that person, just to have him/her rip our hearts out from inside our chests and walk away. Many people still believe that there are levels of severity for which you are allowed to feel heartbroken.

Marriage > long-term relationships > short-term relationships > casual partners > friends with benefits > crushes

But this is not the case at all, and the more we try to tell ourselves that it is and believe that other people's heartbreaks are more "severe" than ours because of the length of their relationships, the more we end up hurting ourselves.

We need to stop lying to ourselves that we are not in pain.

Crazy & Obsessed
Addicted to Relationships

We need to stop trying to quickly heal ourselves from losing the ones we love by having mindless sex with or serially dating other people.

We need to stop covering our true pain with fake smiles so others think we are okay.

We need to stop pretending that we are okay when we are not.

Even more so, we need to stop obsessing over the ones we have lost and bombarding them with every thought that pops into our heads. That may have been alright to do at one point IN THE RELATIONSHIP, but when someone wants out of a relationship, for any reason, valid or invalid, stupid or not, we need to learn to accept that and let that person go.

I am not innocent or logical when it comes to breakups, and my impulsivity can turn me from a sweet and caring girlfriend to a crazy and psychotic bitch who does not know how to accept rejection and move on.

I go back and forth with hating my exes.

Loving them.

Apologizing for actions I have not committed.

Begging for forgiveness and second chances.

Accepting responsibility for all faults of the relationships.

Telling myself that I am better off without them.

Crazy & Obsessed
Addicted to Relationships

Denying the reality of the situations.

Attempting to move on by dating the next person I run into.

Becoming angry and hostile when pleads to my exes do not work.

Becoming depressed and borderline.

Sitting in my apartment for months, drinking, binging, and hating the world.

Completely losing myself.

Being desperate and heartbroken make us ignore what is going on. We become addicted to reaching out to our exes and the idea of our exes rather than wanting to be with them. Our addictions blind us from what we want and keep us focused on one goal: TO GET THEM BACK.

We think that by making dumb compromises and promises we do not believe in, they will come running back to us and pleading to be with us.

But when does that ever happen? The more dumb compromises and fake promises that we make, the more we drive them away, and we know that, BUT WE STILL DO THEM ANYWAY. This is life, and life likes to fuck with us by giving us what we do not want and taking away the things we love most.

Haven't you ever realized that when your ex-partner, the same ex-partner you have spent months, or even years, crying miserably over, comes back to you ONLY when you are NO LONGER OBSESSING over him/her, you feel instantly turned off, regardless of whether you have met someone new or not, and you no longer want that ex-partner back?

We think we love someone now and that this is the greatest person out there, and in some cases, that may be true, but the person we painfully chase and destroy ourselves over will most likely not be the person we end up with.

Persistence does not equate to love. 99% of us do not end up with our first lovers or the "perfect person." Instead, we end up settling for those who actually stick around, those who love us enough to NOT HURT us. Not even once.

If they are capable of hurting us once, they are capable of hurting us again.

When someone leaves us, we expend all our energy on him/her until we are drained. We then become tired of chasing "the one" and settle for those who treat us like we matter. We do not marry the ones we fall for at first sight, the ones we connect with immediately and have amazing sex with; we marry the ones who treat us the way we deserve to be treated, and we eventually learn to love them.

I firmly believe that, if a relationship does not work out the first time, then it will never be the same the second time around despite how hard we work at it. It may work out in the sense of fewer arguments and more compromises, but the spark, passion, and trust that drove

Crazy & Obsessed
Addicted to Relationships

two people together in the first place will never be recovered.

Once a traitor, always a traitor.

When we commit ourselves to long-term relationships, or when we have learned to trust someone so immensely, we fear letting that go.

We fear not being able to find someone else who understands us and loves us.

We fear starting over.

We fear the idea of trusting someone new because we do not want to be betrayed again.

We fear acknowledging that we have made decisions that ended in failure.

We fear failure.

We all desperately want to love that we generate thoughts we do not believe in like, "we should change for someone else," "this is the best it is going to get," and "it will definitely work out this time!" Human beings crave love and affection. We fall head-over-heels when the ones we love promise to never forsake us or promise to give us the world.

These "promises" strike our core desires so intensely that, from that moment on, we place those people on our pedestals. We become attached to the words of those people rather than the people themselves. We lose ourselves in those relationships as we try to make those partners happy, and we lose ourselves when those relationships are over as we try to get those partners back.

We no longer know who we are.

We are all strong and independent people who had lives of our own before we fell in love, and we strive to continue to have lives even when that love is taken away. However, when heartbreak hits, our hearts drop to the ground, our brains turn into mush, and we become the people we ridicule in romantic movies. When we are heartbroken, we can only focus on trying to get our exes back. We do not take the time to reflect on whether having them back is what we truly want, and we do not know if we still love them. We only know that we want them because we no longer have them.

We want what we cannot have. We need that challenge, and our exes thrive on that. We give them power when we chase after them, and they hold onto that power when they refuse to acknowledge us. They know that as soon as they answer us or hint that they want us back, we stop chasing, and ALL EXES LOVE BEING CHASED.

This is also why exes always come back AS SOON AS we stop chasing. Like I said, human beings want what they cannot have, and they will go crazy until they get it.

Why is it difficult for people to form faithful relationships without craving infidelity or drama?

Why is it difficult for people to compromise without maintaining stubbornness?

Crazy & Obsessed
Addicted to Relationships

Why is it difficult for people to stop fucking with our emotions so they can feel satisfied and powerful?

Why is it difficult for people to stop expecting us to prove our love to them daily?

Why is it difficult for people to stop manipulating others into romantic love?

Chapter Three

If Relationships Are Forced, They Are Not Based On Love

"People can only love us if they want to love us. If we attempt to control opinionated minds, they will eventually rebel and destroy us." ℒ

Have you ever tried to force someone to love you?

Of course!

Has it ever worked?

Crazy & Obsessed
Addicted to Relationships

Hell no!

Why not?

Because love cannot be forced, and no one wants to love, nor be loved, solely out of obligation and pity.

I am guilty of trying to force my exes to stay with me after my breakups. I get anxious that I would lose them forever if I let the breakups run their course. However, forcing someone to love us only drives them away.

If it is meant to be, set them free, and they will come back.

If they truly care about you, they know how to find you.

If they do not, then they do not deserve to be in your life.

Do not waste the best years of your life on someone who is wasting theirs on someone else.

Do you want that?

Do you want to throw away your peak years on someone who barely knows you exist?

When people break up with you, say they need "space," say their feelings for you are gone, or say they no longer see a future with you, BELIEVE THEM! Take the three weeks that you need to spit out every word vomit of pain you have toward them (in the solitude of your own home), but when those subside, just let them go.

Crazy & Obsessed
Addicted to Relationships

FOR THE LOVE OF GOD, DO NOT CHASE SOMEONE WHO TELLS YOU THAT THERE IS NO FUTURE.

Do what you need to get all the shit you have out of your system, but do not, I repeat, DO NOT, let your exes know that you have been miserable without them! If you do not already look pathetic in their minds, you DEFINITELY WILL if you tell them that you have been locked up in your basement for the past three weeks, crying about how much you miss them while listening to Taylor Swift and how much you wish you could see them.

KEEP IT TOGETHER! Please DO NOT be that person who obsessively emails, texts, calls, or shows up at your ex's home or work unannounced!

I have been there.

I have done all of that.

I have locked my phone in a safe to avoid texting, just to break open the latch ten minutes later.

I have forced a friend to take my phone, just to fight her into giving it back.

I have traveled four hours to sit in the parking lot of my ex's workplace, just to be ignored.

I have skipped work to sit outside my ex's apartment until he came home from vacation, just to have him walk right by me.

Crazy & Obsessed
Addicted to Relationships

I have frantically texted my ex's family to try to relay my messages to him through them.

I have smashed my phone to prevent the urge to call my exes. (And no, deleting numbers never work because we always manage to find them, either through billing statements, mutual friends, social media, or work, school, and city directories, and we memorize them to the point where it becomes the only number we can recite.)
I have done it all.

Trust me.

You do not want to go there.

It feels like shit, and it makes you want to crawl into a hole and die!

You are beautiful!

DO NOT die on me!

DO NOT become the stalker who makes your exes proud of their decisions to walk away.

Be the person who is STRONG enough to walk away.

Make your exes regret leaving you!

When they do regret it, DO NOT take them back!

Anyone who can crush us once, can always crush us again.

Crazy & Obsessed
Addicted to Relationships

What happens when the people we desperately want back find other romantic partners to replace us and move on? What is the point of going "no contact" in hopes of getting them back when they are happy with other people?

This is especially true for short-term relationships that have only lasted a few short months. To us, these short-term exes feel like the loves of our lives, and we would do anything to get them back. But to them, we are just another "fling" on their journey toward finding suitable long-term partners.

This truth is hard to swallow. The relationship JUST ended, and they are already posting selfies with someone else while we are still plotting ways to get them back, begging, compromising, and sending them gifts in hopes that they will see the mistakes they have made.

Sadly, but unsurprisingly, they do not give a rat's ass about any of it. They do not care if we feel like hell or if we are miserable and depressed without them.

If you have only been dating someone for a few weeks and have not stopped harassing that person with calls and text messages since the breakup, that person will most likely shut you out of his/her life, completely forgetting who you are after a few months.

When people decide to leave us, there is nothing we can do to GENUINELY make them change their mind.

Chapter Four

Time To Let Go

"Why hold onto something that is broken when it slowly dissolves in our palm with every passing second? If we set the dust free, maybe one day, it will find its way home." ℒ

If someone walks into your life, deceives and lies, and then wants to walk into the arms of someone else, just let go.

Chasing after someone who does not want us is one of the most crushing experiences we can deal with because

Crazy & Obsessed
Addicted to Relationships

we lose all value in both our eyes and theirs. We end up destroying our own lives for someone who is still going to move on regardless of how miserable we are.

It does not matter how great the relationship was, perfect or flawed, successful or failing, if someone's mind is already made up about leaving, it is going to happen, and anything we try to do to prevent that will only catalyze the process.

As much as I still care for the people who have walked in and out of my life, I have learned, the hard way, that even if we care about some people, they are not worth pursuing if we sacrifice our own mental well-beings in the process. If people truly cared for us, they would be preventing, not instigating, our sufferings.

They would make it a priority to NOT hurt us and to NOT leave us (and none of that crap where they come back after being away for six months, and we suddenly believe that they love us again).

Exes usually only come back because they have tried to find someone else and failed, or because they crave the chase and attention we shower them with. They say all the right things and make us feel like the most special people in the world so we will take them back. They call us every night (for a few weeks) and tell us how they cannot wait to spend their futures with us, making us fall in love all over again.

Then, they take it all away and pretend like we are nonexistent again. We are not idiots; we are successful scientists, doctors, lawyers, entrepreneurs, and leaders of the world, but for some reason, we become incredibly dumb and ignorant when it comes to love.

Is love worth chasing?

Yes.

Just not love from those who have already taken it away from us.

I am not advertising dating every seemingly nice and unattractive person in attempts to find the one you are destined to marry.

I am also not advertising proposing to the next person who offers you a slice a pizza, although that certainly makes it easier.

I am not even advertising that you NEED a partner in order to find love.

We all crave the idea of love, but what is love? How do we find love? We hear influencers and advocates say, "We must love ourselves before we can love others or before we can expect others to love us."

However, many people misinterpret this saying. TRULY LOVING OURSELVES does not mean buying five Prada handbags, getting brand-new faces, or acting like egotistical assholes who do not have time to be decent human beings because we are too busy "loving ourselves." Truly loving means figuring out WHAT love means to us.

Crazy & Obsessed
Addicted to Relationships

Love is a subjective term, and the more time we spend defining love under the generic definition of "being with our soulmates and living happily ever after," the more time we take away from discovering what it means to US.

Love can have many meanings, from loyalty and acceptance to non-judgmental thoughts and honesty to friendship and humor. We cannot rush what love means because it will appear when we ALLOW it to appear. There are many people, especially those in their late 20s to early 40s, who believe they MUST FIND LOVE NOW, or they will end up old and alone.

How can we let love in if we hyper-focus on PRETENDING to be in "love" with people we have only known for two weeks?

How can we decide whether people are right for us and propose marriage based on a couple of months?

Why do we automatically assume people are not right for us as soon as complications occur?

We like to judge relationships based on feelings. If we feel positive emotions toward someone, we stay. If not, we leave. Simple, right? Not at all, and we need to stop destroying relationships and the lives of others based solely on how we feel.

Seriously, just stop.

Feelings change all the time based on what is going on in our lives at specific moments. Stress makes us hate everyone while joy makes us love. Stop making impulsive decisions to break up with our partners because we are mad at them for being late or because their choices do not currently align with ours.

"My feelings for you have changed." A classic breakup line. Just because we are not in the honeymoon phase anymore and our infatuations have turned to content, does not mean that it is time to throw in the towel and call it quits. We cannot be head-over-heels for someone all the time, and there will always be obstacles that change how we feel toward the other person at any given moment.

We cannot judge how a relationship is going after only a couple of months. How can we be so sure that the relationship will not work out when we are only starting to get to know a person?

Most relationships need at least six months before two people can figure out each other's likes and dislikes, and determine if they can compromise with each other on issues that could potentially arise.

Sadly, when our feelings begin to fade, the person we crush on also fades, and we move onto finding someone else. It is a shallow perception, but in the moment, we make up excuses as to why we do it, and we justify breaking off what could potentially turn out to be great before giving it a chance to get there.

We tell ourselves that what we feel in specific moments is what we will feel forever toward that person, and we run before giving the relationship a chance to play out.

When our minds become congested with opposing feelings and overwhelming anxiety, we train ourselves to narrow our focus toward one dichotomous aspect: to give or not to give.

We refuse to compromise when our feelings take over, and we become stubborn to any ideas that go against our own. Relationships are hard, but unfortunately, many still believe that if it is not easy during the beginning stages, then the person is not worth pursuing at all.

This mentality causes us to hurt people because we blindsight them. We lead them to believe that they mean everything to us, and that we are completely happy with them, while holding back our true feelings.

Maybe it is due to the fear of trusting someone and potentially getting hurt.

Maybe it is due to the fear of hurting someone's feelings.

Maybe we are just not ready.

Not being completely honest and open from the start does more harm than good. If there are doubts early on, speak up! If there is no spark, say something! Let the other person know whether changes can be made to improve the relationship or if it is time to end it. Trust me, it hurts far less to be honest than to lead someone on when you clearly know that there is no future.

We lie and ghost people because we are afraid of dealing with their pain.

We feel guilty when our actions hurt someone.

Crazy & Obsessed
Addicted to Relationships

We find it easier to deal with hurting someone by removing ourselves from them rather than acknowledging their pain.

We ghost, we block, and we completely ignore people we used to care so deeply for because we are not strong enough to carry their sufferings.

We fail to realize that we can relieve a lot of their pain with simple honesty.

Share every part of who you are.

Share all your thoughts, your doubts, your issues, your likes, and your burdens.

If someone is meant to be in your life, they will accept you for who you are despite your baggage.

Why hide parts of who you are?

Why be ashamed of showing your true self just because you think you are different?

Why change the person you were born to be just to please the selfish needs of others?

Relationships based on lies and secrets never last. If we expose ourselves completely, we can filter those who will stick around from those who will eventually break our spirits. Although heartbreak is inevitable, we can still avoid regret when a relationship, long or short, ends because we know that the end was based on incompatibility rather than something we controlled.

Crazy & Obsessed
Addicted to Relationships

We cannot control or change the actions of others.

We can only express how we are affected by their actions.

We can only control our own actions in response to others.

We cannot force others to love us, but we can force ourselves to love us.

People walk in and out of our lives every day for all different reasons. Even compassionate people have their moments and can surprise us by leaving.

A good friend once told me that you must be prepared for anything and everything.

We should not put ourselves in positions where we feel vulnerable to another person and give them so much power over us that, when they betray us, we completely crumble. Even if it feels comfortable and familiar to depend on someone other than ourselves, NO ONE SHOULD HAVE THAT KIND OF CONTROL over our lives.

We are the only ones we can trust completely. Even our family and friends can forsake us and leave us dry. Spouses leave all the time despite committed vows. We can spend 60+ years with people, commit to sharing every part of our lives with them, and STILL RISK them walking away.

Even if they are still physically present, mental separation hurts just as much when we realize there is almost nothing we can say or do to bring them back. It kills us to know that the people who used to say "I love you" to us are now secretly hating every part of our existences, but, just as we chase people who leave us, we also chase people who resent us. The desire to want love and connection can feel so strong that we often put up with abuse and neglect.

Note: FEELING like we are still with someone is NOT the same as BEING with someone.

We refuse to accept that the people we love can actively choose to remove themselves from our lives, and we hold onto the fantasy of what used to be and let those memories drive us toward physical and emotional abuse.

Memories of the "happier times" and thoughts of "what could have been" force us to ignore reality and put abusers on pedestals when they do not deserve it. We fault and blame ourselves for causing others to hurt us, and we take full responsibility for our sufferings regardless of who is at fault.

We cannot blame ourselves for feeling hurt, and we cannot blame ourselves for being emotional.

As human beings, we naturally feel pain. Just because there are certain societal standards on how we SHOULD feel and react after someone breaks our hearts, does not mean that we are obligated to follow them. No one has the right to tell us how to feel nor do we have the right to tell others how to feel.

We question whether we have done everything "right" during the relationship.

Crazy & Obsessed
Addicted to Relationships

We question if we could have done more.

We question whether the relationship ended because of us.

We usually believe that it did.

We question what we could do now to redeem ourselves.

We question if the relationship is a lost cause.

We question our self-worth and whether we deserve happiness.

We question if anyone will ever love us again.

Why is it so easy for us to obsess over, chase, and give our worlds to others, but so difficult for us to do the same to ourselves?

Why do we believe that it is selfish to obsess over our own happiness by splurging on ourselves?

Why do we frown upon taking ourselves out on dates?

Why is it only socially acceptable to go out on dates with partners?

Why do we hurt ourselves when someone else is already doing it?

Why do we become stubborn and childish when someone does not want to be with us?

It is because we LOVE too much.

Crazy & Obsessed
Addicted to Relationships

We fight for people and for relationships that we care about even if the fight destroys us. We deceive ourselves into believing that chasing after someone is a sign of love, compassion, and strength, but doing so only implies weakness and narcissism.

We become so hurt by the relationship that we try to compensate by acting like saints, professing our love and affection when the other person just wants out. The only way we can truly be "saints" is if we let go.

As hard as it is to not reach out to someone we love, it is the only non-selfish act we can do.

Keep in mind that I DO NOT mean not reaching out for the sake of manipulation. I mean not reaching out for the sake of letting go and letting those we love make their own decisions, letting those we love choose who they want to be with, and not forcing them to love us when they can barely look at us.

I need to let him go.

We all need to let them go.

Stop torturing ourselves by loving someone who refuses to love us back.

They might come back.

They might not.

But we cannot hold onto the belief that they will.

That belief will tear our lives apart.

Crazy & Obsessed
Addicted to Relationships

That belief will take away our sanity, happiness, and youth.

We should not be hoping that our days end quicker so we can bypass our no contact periods.

We should not be living for others.

We had lives before we fell in love.

We still have lives when love dies.

As challenging as it is to not feel angry, miserable, depressed, or suicidal after the loss of someone, we must.

We must continue living.

Do not give anyone else the power to control our lives.

If we do, we will always regret it.

Trust me.

YOU WILL REGRET IT.

Chapter Five

We Are All Affected

"We need to stop believing that we will never be flawed, stop believing that we will never encounter problems, stop believing that we will never be pained by what pains others. Beliefs are no match for the wrath of life."
ℒ

As humans, our emotions change all the time. The sadness that comes from heartbreak can quickly turn into happiness from finding new love, which can quickly turn into depression from the loss of a parent, which can quickly turn into excitement from traveling somewhere new.

We are emotional creatures, and therefore, we can never predict how we will behave in different situations. We may call ourselves "calm," "patient," and "collected," and we may have even discovered a pattern in our reactions based on various experiences, but every circumstance is different, every day is different, and every time we interact with a situation, similar setting or not, we are presented with a new challenge.

Our emotional presence, the relationships we have with those around us, our current living situations, and our current satisfaction with life all dictate how we react to specific situations that occur at specific moments.

Many of us have been dumped, yet many of us get back together. Hell, many of us cycle through on-and-off relationships so much that we struggle with getting out when we want to. However, the reason we are stuck is because the problems that caused the relationships to initially fail never get resolved. Therefore, we become crazy, devastated, and heartbroken, and we swear to ourselves that we will never look back.

But we go back anyway.

We fight.

We break up.

We become crazy, devastated, and heartbroken once again.

Crazy & Obsessed
Addicted to Relationships

Until we are fed up.

And we begin obsessing over someone else.

The cycle continues.

Until we finally meet someone who will stay.

Someone who will love us.

Someone who will always be there.

The someone we have been searching for all these years.

And we leave.

Because we struggle with our own happiness.

Someone is always the victim.

Someone always loses.

Even mutual splits are never actually mutual.

One person always feels more than the other.

One person always moves on quicker than the other.

We are victims in some relationships.

We are heartbreakers in others.

Emotions are messy.

No one can truly know what they want or who they want.

Crazy & Obsessed
Addicted to Relationships

Some of us still confuse love with infatuation.

Some of us cheat on those we love because of moments of weakness.

We crave acceptance and companionship all the time.

When we cannot get them from the ones we are currently with, we seek them out in others.

Friends.

Colleagues.

Exes.

Strangers.

Anyone.

We become obsessed with our new "loves" because we believe they are everything that our current partners are not. We base our entire relationships on a few bad moments and use them as excuses to be unfaithful. We fall in "love" with people we have just met because we compare their positives to our partners' negatives. But, when the new "relationship" falls apart, we blame them for not being as good.

We do not know what the fuck we want.

New relationships never thrive when we are stuck in the old. We end up becoming too attached too soon, and we scare them away. We start comparing them to our pasts, and we fault them when they do not measure up.

Crazy & Obsessed
Addicted to Relationships

If you ever wonder why you are still single, see if you notice a pattern when it comes to meeting new people.

I know I am not alone when I say I would rather throw my phone into a lake and crawl into a hole than face another 96-hour day staring at my phone with no messages from my ex and more pictures of him with his new catch. IT HAS ONLY BEEN TWO DAYS! Every minute of every day becomes a debilitating struggle when the one person we need is the only person we cannot have, and it makes us doubt every word, every action, and every decision we have ever made when we were with that person.

We meticulously reflect on all the mistakes we could have avoided to prevent that person from leaving, and we blame every second of bad choices on ourselves. We hate ourselves for letting the "perfect" person walk away, and we hate ourselves for continuing to engage in acts that keep them away.

If he cared, he would have stayed.

If he loved me, he would try to compromise.

He was not right for me.

There was nothing I could have done to make him stay if he wanted out.

If I must change how I am for someone, he is not worth my time.

But we do not believe in these clichés' sayings, do we? When we are in a state of grief and resentment, nothing can pull us out, and it is draining! What used to make us happy no longer do, and depression begins to close in behind.

The people we used to call our "friends" and "family" are now seen as a nuisance when they try to help.

The world around us becomes our enemy.

We become bitter and angry when we see others in love.

We slap on fake smiles to hide our miseries.

We are dying from the inside out.

Heartbreak destroys lives and perceptions become clouded.

We begin to hate when we used to love.

We become selfish and angry when we used to be sweet and kind.

We become crazy and obsessive when we used to be independent and strong.

Our entire world flips, and we no longer recognize who we are.

Whether we are male or female, whether we fit society's standards of attraction and intelligence, whether we are the "dumper" or the "dumpee," whether the relationship was long or short, and whether we were in love or just pretending, heartbreak cripples all of us equally.

Crazy & Obsessed
Addicted to Relationships

We all experience the same devastating shatter in our hearts when a lost occurs.

It pains us when the people we used to call our "lights" now become our enemies.

It pains us when we no longer have the support system we have had for years.

It pains us when the people we used to love now see us as strangers.

How do we deal with this pain?

How do we breathe when our minds cannot fathom reality?

How do we wake up every morning when the depression weighs us down?

How do we "get over it and move on"?

We are told to love ourselves instead, but how do we do that?

What if we no longer know what it means to love ourselves because we have spent all our time loving others?

What if our overwhelming fears make us incapable of ever loving again?

We look at others and wonder how they get over heartbreak. We envy those who seem to heal by the snap of a finger. But are they healed? Are they really over their heartbreaks, or are they just that good at hiding their pain? We live in a world where we must pretend to be strong, where we must pretend to be resilient in the face of obstacles, and where we must walk outside with our shits held together and the biggest smiles slapped on our faces or risk being judged for having problems. God forbid that humans beings have problems!

We all have issues in our lives, but we still judge those around us for having the same issues. We are hypocrites. We hold others to double standards. We are intelligent enough to know the consequences of our actions, but we are also too proud to admit our flaws. We believe that by meddling in the lives of others and giving them advice that we do not believe in, then we can pretend that our own struggles do not exist.

We trick ourselves into believing that we are "perfect" while everyone else is flawed. We run and hide from ourselves all the time. We run from our therapists by withholding full disclosure. We say just enough to be medicated but not enough to be hospitalized.

We lie to everyone around us.

We lie to ourselves.

We do not know how to be honest with ourselves. The ones who say they do are only admitting the parts that they want to admit, and the ones who embark on "spiritual journeys" to "find themselves" only do so for bragging rights. We do not need to spend $4,000 in India on a yoga retreat to gain "honesty within," and we do not need to hike across the country or strand ourselves in the middle of the woods to "find ourselves."

Crazy & Obsessed
Addicted to Relationships

Just.

Stop.

Running.

Only by admitting that we are crazy, stupid, obsessive, impulsive, manipulative, and psychotic can we finally begin to move forward with our lives, away from fear. We may not want to admit our flaws to other people, but what harm is there by admitting the truth to ourselves? We cannot possibly judge ourselves more than we already do.

We are already our own worst enemies so we have nothing more to lose. But we still hold back! We are so afraid of ourselves and our thoughts that we cannot even admit to ourselves what nobody else needs to know!

What is wrong with us?

Why are we so afraid of our negative sides?

We try so hard to become the qualities that are "favorable" and "attractive" while shoving everything else inside a box.

And that, my friends, is why we drink.

That is why we let pain and anger unleash the dark sides of us.

Because we will then have something to blame other than ourselves.

Crazy & Obsessed
Addicted to Relationships

We let our emotions and external factors speak what we cannot communicate through words.

Chapter Six

Society Dooms Us All

"We cannot call ourselves 'independent' when we abide by the rules of others; it is an oxymoron." ℒ

Every single one of us is a scared, timid, and angry child, afraid of rejection, loneliness, pain, and anxiety, who pretends to be mature adults with our lives put together because then, and only then, will we be accepted as functional members of society rather than social outcasts. We reject those who do not fit in with the norm.

Crazy & Obsessed
Addicted to Relationships

For example, on dating apps, no one chooses to like and connect with those who are disabled and uneducated. We swipe left on those who do not meet our standard of attractiveness because they do not meet society's standard of attractiveness, and by dating them, we, by default, also become rejected by society.

We cast aside those who do not fit the mold, and we ignore how we may have just hurt people we really liked just because everyone else refused to accept them, and because of that, we do not apologize, we do not acknowledge, and we do not communicate; we just block.

The rules of dating and love that others have set for us make us lose control of our own minds. We believe that we are in control of ourselves and that we are the "pilot of our own lives," but when we blindly follow what we are SUPPOSED to do rather than what we WANT to do, we give up that control, and we allow those around us to dictate who we love, who we can accept into our lives, and who we can talk to.

We let society tell us that we can no longer acknowledge that our exes, despite how long the relationships were, ever existed. We force ourselves to treat someone we used to love as strangers because it is not socially acceptable to keep in contact with an ex-partner as it prevents us from healing and moving on.

While it is true that keeping in constant contact with someone who we can no longer love prolongs our pain and keeps us from moving on, it becomes cruel and unnecessary to just shut them out completely.

Crazy & Obsessed
Addicted to Relationships

How would you like it if someone did that to you?

We do not have to talk to them every day, like we used to in the relationships, but we also do not have to actively ignore them and block them either. We try to manipulate people's feelings by enforcing the dumb "No Contact Rule," deleting their numbers, ignoring them, blocking them, and doing everything we possibly can to remove them from our lives, that we fail to realize that we are still hurting human beings.

When we are hurt or angry, we can only focus on ourselves.

We only want to focus on ourselves.

We fail to notice the feelings of the people on the other end of our pain when we are trying to repair ourselves.

We fail to realize that we are actively bringing down the confidence levels and self-esteem of others just so we can bring them up in ourselves.

We only realize how much we are hurting the people we care about AFTER the damage has already been done.

Chapter Seven

We Never Get Over It

"We can run away all we want, as much as we want. I did, but if we never address what we are running from, we are only pulling it along for the journey." 𝓛

Imagine a couple of months after the breakup, where we actually do say "fuck you" to everything and start feeling okay again. We start feeling like we can finally walk outside with confidence and go entire days without thinking about our exes. We learn how to enjoy a cup of coffee or a nice dinner out alone, without the company of another person.

Crazy & Obsessed
Addicted to Relationships

Then we find out our exes are dating again, and all hell breaks loose. To make it worse, they have the audacity to TELL US about their new dating life.

What the fuck do they expect from us by telling us that? Are we supposed to say, "Congratulations on finding my replacement and completely forgetting the fucking life we had together!"? It is hard enough when people move on, and it is okay that they do, but when they decide to drag us along for the ride, making us suffer even more as they move on, that is just deceitful.

Decent human beings cut off contact with their exes when they start dating new people, to not offend the new and to not mess with the old. Narcissistic people, on the other hand, intentionally tell everyone about what they are doing because they know it will hurt, and narcissists thrive on the misery of others.

Narcissists want attention. They know EXACTLY what to say to piss us off and get the reactions they want out of us. ANY reaction we give them, even saying "fuck you," will only fuel them because that shows them that we still care enough to respond. The only thing that can hurt a narcissist is complete silence. As much anger, sadness, pain, and hate we have toward them, do not let them know!

And what do we do?

We have one moment of weakness, and WE LET THEM KNOW.

That is when they have us hooked.

Crazy & Obsessed
Addicted to Relationships

When we let people in, we leave our vulnerabilities open and allow them to hurt us.

When we welcome the chance to love and trust others, we also welcome the chance to become physically and emotionally crushed.

Humans are resilient.

Believe it or not.

It feels like shit when someone leaves.

It feels like shit when someone decides we are no longer worth it.

It feels like shit when we invest so much of ourselves into something, just to watch it all fall apart.

But feeling like shit is just an emotion.

Just like feeling in love is just an emotion.

Emotions are always changing.

One minute, we can be in love.

The next minute, we can decide that we hate our partners.

That is why divorce is so common. We trick ourselves into believing that we are in love even when we are not. We do not realize that this feeling of "love" is simply a fleeting emotion that can change just as quickly as we change our clothes. When we FEEL in love, we get married. But just as easily, when we FEEL angry or hatred, we get divorced, walk away, or become unfaithful.

We are impulsive creatures, and we take major actions based on fleeting feelings. However, the lesson here is, emotions and feelings come and go! Even if we feel like we do not want to live anymore after the end of a relationship, or if we feel like we will never get over the pain, we will, because we all eventually do!

Whether we find love in someone else or something else, we WILL move past the heartbreak, and years down the line, we will look back at our painful moments and realize how much of our lives we have wasted on JUST a feeling.

Note: I am not saying this is time wasted on the relationship or time wasted on the person. I am saying time wasted on a FEELING, something that we create and can easily remove, something that is a part of us, but does not define us.

Chapter Eight

Identity Crisis

"Sometimes I wonder what life would be like if I was perfect, if I made no mistakes, if I was just like everyone else, and if I did not possess one single flaw. Then I realize, I would be a robot." ℒ

We let our pain, our guilt, our fear, our happiness and sadness, our anger, and our anxiety drive our lives, and we begin to define ourselves based on how we feel rather than who we are. When someone asks us who we are as people, most of us tend to say, "I am a wife," "I am an optimist," "I am a forgiver," "I am a risk-taker," etc. These labels all stem from our emotions.

We say we are someone's spouse or partner because we FEEL loved. We say we are an optimist because our lives are currently going well, and we FEEL happy as a result of it. We say we live to forgive because we are either lying and want to give off the appearance that we are good people, or because we FEEL tremendous amounts of guilt when we do not forgive those who hurt us.

We say we are risk-takers, not because we are not afraid of dying, which is a common misconception with risk-takers, but because we are afraid of not living. We skydive, swim with sharks, climb Mount Everest, camp out in the woods for months with minimal supplies, and backpack to the most dangerous cities in the world, not because we are brave and fearless, but because we fear the idea of dying without having lived a full life.

We risk our lives for adventure and excitement, whether by jumping off a plane or having an affair, because we FEEL afraid that the monotonous lives we are currently living will be how we live until we die, and that is SCARY!

We overcome obstacles because we fear being dull and boring, not because we are courageous and adventurous. We live in a constant state of comparison, where we feel like we must be "different" even though we are all doing the same things to achieve that difference. Who are we trying to please? Our parents? Our friends? Social media? Who are they to say that our lives now are not enough?

NOBODY!

Crazy & Obsessed
Addicted to Relationships

But we try anyway! We literally die trying to live up to the standards of "living life to the fullest." We freeze on top of mountains because we believe we "must climb to avoid failure." We plummet to our deaths by jumping off planes because, for some oxymoronic reason, we associate near-death with living life.

I am guilty of falling for these gimmicks myself, and I have tried to convince myself that these are my unique wants and desires even though they are the same as everybody else's. That does not make me unique! That makes me just as gullible as everyone else, but I still do not stop.

I continue falling for the lies of needing to put my life at risk in order to live. I continue falling for the lies of terrible decisions being fantastic ideas because that is the mentality I am forced to acknowledge.

This is what relationships are. As I mentioned before, human beings are intelligent creatures, far more intelligent than we give ourselves credit for, but human beings are also very gullible, and because of that, we become very stupid. Deep down, we know we must work on our own lives and figure out our own issues before we can even think about bringing a partner into our mess. We know that, when a relationship is terrible and it makes us feel depressed, then it means it is time to walk away.

We know that there is only so much we can do in a relationship before realizing that it just is not going to work. But, the more we realize the emotionally dangerous situations that we put ourselves in, the more we try to avoid facing them.

Crazy & Obsessed
Addicted to Relationships

Why? Two reasons. We avoid acknowledging that our terrible relationships are terrible, and we avoid getting out of them because we are SCARED and/or STUBBORN.

We do not want to admit that we have failed in something we invested so much of our lives in.

We are afraid that no one else will love us so we would rather stay in a failed relationship than no relationship at all.

We are too proud to face our friends and family because they will flaunt in our faces how they told us the relationship was not right, but we decided to pursue it anyway.

We are scared of being left behind when everyone our age is moving forward, getting married, and having babies while we are still stuck in our parents' basement, eating cookie dough out of a tube in our pajamas, so we snatch and settle for the first, potentially abusive, suitor for face value, to show that we are adults and not a 10-year-old inside a 35-year old's body.

We lie to ourselves and everyone else that we are okay with physical and mental abuse from our partners because we are "in love," and "love overcomes everything."

While love can overcome petty fights, stress, financial struggles, and in some cases, infidelity, how many of us can stick by this belief when we are:

Lying, half-dead, in a hospital bed,

Crazy & Obsessed
Addicted to Relationships

Ripping our hairs out until we create bald patches,

Driving aimlessly in the middle of the night, afraid to go home because we might get beat,

Forcing ourselves to look and feel ugly just to ease our lovers' insecurities, while damaging our own confidences,

Hating ourselves when we look in the mirror,

Or, taking a gun to our heads but afraid to shoot because we feel guilty for acting selfishly?

I, like many others who have been in abusive relationships, have had these thoughts once or twice before.

We struggle between hating and loving our partners.

We struggle between leaving and staying.
Those of us who fear for our lives still contemplate this decision.

We go back and forth so many times that we eventually drive ourselves insane.

We give up trying.

We stay in the relationships.

We become depressed.

Chapter Nine

Innocent Abusers

"Do not chastise them for being themselves; they do not know the pain they cause." 𝓛

Sometimes, the abusers are innocent. Yes, I said it. There are some abusers who are aware of what they are doing with no intention of stopping; these are usually the physical abusers. Then we have the emotional abusers, the more common type, where the question of whether they are guilty or innocent falls more in the grey area than the dichotomous black and white.

Crazy & Obsessed
Addicted to Relationships

Because we are each our own individuals, we have different upbringings, personalities, culture, values, beliefs, standards, and definitions of what it means to be in a relationship. Hence, while our words and actions may not seem offensive and abusive to us, they can to someone else.

Think of it in terms of a culture shock. Norms in the western part of the world are seen as insults in the eastern part of the world. For example, it is customary to tip the waiter after service in most western countries, but when that is done in eastern countries, waiters become offended, and they literally chase you down to give you your money back.

In healthy relationships, those who feel triggered or offended by their partners' words or actions often speak up and let their partners know, and thus, the partners stop. However, this can become abusive when we either refuse to speak out due to shame and embarrassment, or we do speak out but the other person dismisses us because our values do not align with theirs.

The more people dismiss our feelings, the more we need to speak out and let them know; otherwise, they keep repeating the action because we keep letting them.

People can be incredibly slow and terrible listeners, and this is not an excuse for them, but when we encounter these situations, mentioning only once or twice that our feelings have been hurt and then failing to remain consistent, this only portrays the idea that we were never serious or hurt in the first place.

Crazy & Obsessed
Addicted to Relationships

Ladies! Gentlemen! We need our voices and our feelings to be heard! No one can speak our souls for us, and no one will ever understand us unless we make ourselves be known. And no, none of the bullshit, "It must be true love because he/she understands me in a way that no one else ever has."

No! Unless this person has telekinesis, or is a troll living inside your brain and your heart, the only person who will ever understand you more than you is YOU!

You are probably thinking, "How can I understand me more than me if I am me? This is a paradox!" Maybe it is. Maybe this is a dream and none of the words you are reading exist. Or maybe, as stated previously, human beings are complex creatures. We are in constant discovery of ourselves and of the world.

Every day we are learning:

Learning about our likes and our dislikes as we experience new encounters,

Learning about how we react to different people in different situations,

Learning about how others react to us based on our specific behaviors,

Learning about why some people like us while others dislike us,

Learning about why we like some people and dislike others,

Crazy & Obsessed
Addicted to Relationships

And, learning about how we are compatible with everyone and but also compatible with no one.

We never fully establish who we are or what we want from others. We are so spontaneous and unpredictable that it is rare that we find people who want the same things or behave the same ways their entire lives. Breakups and divorces do not happen because two people hate each other; they happen because one person in the relationship has changed their wants. This change can happen within years, months, or even days.

From personal experience, I have been with someone who went from worshipping the ground I step on to wanting absolutely nothing to do with me within a span of two hours. Although I did not know his thoughts and perceptions of me during the short month we have been together, I do know that his feelings have changed, whether sudden or not.

From his perspective, his thoughts and actions may make complete sense, but I am speaking from my perspective:

The perspective of those on the receiving end,

The perspective of those who blame themselves because of the rejection and confusion other people have caused,

The perspective of those who never receive an explanation or closure from the end of relationships,

And, the perspective that ultimately leads people to end their lives because heartbreak can literally kill us, mentally and physically.

Crazy & Obsessed
Addicted to Relationships

Feelings change sporadically due to faults of no one, but we do not see the change. Instead, we see the result and blame ourselves for being the cause.

How many times have we said or heard someone else say,

"Losing you makes me feel so depressed and miserable that I no longer have a reason to live,"

"I will never feel happy again without you,"

And, "Without you, I feel like I am nothing."

These are all feelings caused by the pain of breakups or divorces, not necessarily due to anyone's fault since this can arise even from mutual breakups, which is a topic in its own league that I will touch upon later, but we always try to rationalize where these painful feelings come from. We can never truly understand that we can feel different emotions because our brains are wired to do so, and feelings can be triggered by even the smallest of things.

We can never just say, "I feel like shit right now, but it is just a feeling, and tomorrow I may have a different feeling." We rationalize our feelings, in that if we cannot blame the feeling on something or someone, then we should not be feeling it because it is "not acceptable."

In our society, we are only allowed positivity and optimism. We must be happy all the time or there is something "wrong" with us. Millions seek out therapy because we trick ourselves into believing that any ounce of sadness or pain that we experience is a problem that must be treated.

Crazy & Obsessed
Addicted to Relationships

We cannot fix something that is a natural part of us, and attempting to do so will only cause unnecessary stress, anxiety, guilt, regret, and, ultimately, more pain.

Unfortunately, on the flip side, feeling too happy and too optimistic can also be seen as "problems." If we seem too happy, we are either defined as "manic" or "abnormal." If we seem too optimistic, we are either defined as "sheltered" or "privileged."

Even if we are the "normal" amount of happy, this can still be problematic depending on the people surrounding us. Some may see it as still too much while others may see it as not enough. Either way, we cannot win.

This is the unwritten rule: Be the right amount of enthusiasm and positivity, catering to every person's needs at the same time, and never show any other emotion because any emotion other than happy is frowned upon.

Simple enough.

Right?

Chapter Ten

The Demise Of XY

"Women justify equal rights when they try to take from men what they believe was taken from them. In reality, they are only stealing." ℒ

Many of us have been told that only women are held to high standards. However, men deal with the same pressure as women do because women and men are equally mean and cruel, just as we are both are equally vulnerable to pain and rejection.

Crazy & Obsessed
Addicted to Relationships

We like to categorize men as "dogs," "pigs," and the 50 other animals we call men after they break our hearts. Yes, men lie, cheat, run, and abuse, both verbally and physically, but so do women. In fact, women can sometimes be worse because we usually do not associate domestic abuse with women.

Women are still seen as "weak," "frail," and "victims." Even if a woman repeatedly kicks a man's genitalia, we still defend her by saying she must have been provoked.

Women are just as terrible as men, but do we see movies, magazines, and books catered toward men outlining,

"10 Ways to Find Your Inner Masculinity Again After a Breakup,"

"You are a Beautiful and Independent Angel Without a Woman,"

"Be the Unforgettable Man,"

"Discover your Spiritual Manhood," or

"The Penis Monologues"?

Chapter Eleven

Happy Wife, Happy Life

"Can true happiness really be dependent on one quote, one word, one person? We are all looking out for ourselves; no one cares if you perish." ℒ

This phrase is the epitome of men being brainwashed into taking abuse from women. Most men are willing to bow over for the women they love, despite what it takes, until they reach their breaking points.

But men, try this: leave. As soon as you decide to end a relationship, the women suddenly switch personalities, lose power, and her insecurities begin to show. It does not matter how strong, confident, demanding, or un-gettable someone appears to be.

Everyone is only human, and the only reason these seemingly powerful people got to where they are is because everyone around them enables their behaviors, and the men/women who shower these powerful people with attention, gifts, blood, and tears are only screwing themselves over. It is a common misunderstanding that the more we give to make someone happy, the more likely the other person is to return the favor.

You are laughing too, right?

What really happens is that the more we give and are willing to give, the more others take. Catering to people to make them "happy" only fuels their selfishness. However, because one of the biggest strengths and flaws in human beings is fear, in that fear motivates us to reach for the impossible but also cripples us to hold onto tragic pasts, we are also gullible enough to willingly give up our own lives and our own happiness in hopes that our sacrifices will be rewarded.

Unfortunately, this reward is not the reward of our partners loving us back or the reward of them making sacrifices for our benefits; this reward is the fake lifetime promise of "forever." So, we give up everything we have for each relationship because we fall for these false promises of forever EVERY SINGLE TIME. We search, we drain ourselves, we settle, we resent, we leave, we find someone else, and the entire cycle starts over again until we reach the point where mediocre is good enough.

Crazy & Obsessed
Addicted to Relationships

While finding our soulmates is a great dream to chase, it is not reality. Neither is compatibility. No two people are "meant to be together" because we all have our own opinions, our own ways of living, being, and feeling, and it becomes near impossible to find someone who meets ALL the desires and personalities we look for.

Love exists; I am not against it. I fully believe in finding someone we want to share and dedicate the rest of our lives to. What I do not believe, however, is giving up our own lives solely to benefit the lives of others and failing to see how detrimental it is to do so.

As much as it sucks to say, and sucks even more to believe, people are flakes. It is in our nature to run away from our problems because we are taught to seek out happiness and avoid every other emotion. Therefore, we relish in the happy moments in our relationships, feeling on top of the world, but once life starts to get hard and reality kicks in, we bolt as if Godzilla is chasing us.

We are not wired to deal with hardships. We have been so sheltered and/or privileged that we expect our lives to transition smoothly from one stage to another. We would much rather destroy the life of someone else than face our own insecurities and our unwanted emotions. Epinephrine skyrockets in situations of fear, which in this case is the fear of being unhappy, and we run.

It is rare that we fight for our relationships, and I mean fight in cases like a partner loses his/her job and files for bankruptcy, accidental pregnancy with lack of preparation, or moving to a different country when a partner finds a new job, not in cases like getting mad at our partners for buying us Snickers instead of Milky Way.

Crazy & Obsessed
Addicted to Relationships

Note: If your partner cheats on you in any way, shape, or form, he/she is not worth fighting for.

Humans beings are selfish. We hate compromises, and we hate opinions that do not align with our own. We would much rather leave someone we love than admit that we are wrong. This is why on-and-off relationships are so common. We leave when we are stressed out, angry, or sad, cool down, and then realize how petty we were and how much we love the other person, and beg for him/her to take us back.

Why leave it up to chance? Why throw everything away based on one emotion in hopes that the other person is patient, stupid, or lonely enough to want us back after we turn into assholes and walk away?

Unfortunately, cliché gifts and a slew of false promises are usually enough to win people over even after we crush their hearts. When we want out, we put the other person through hell and make damn sure that he/she never wants a future with us. When we want in, we become sly enough to manipulate the other person into not being able to imagine a future without us, and we literally become a "knight in shining armor" or an "angel sent from heaven."

We are manipulative, and this is one of the greatest strengths of mankind throughout history.

Machiavellianism has existed in our repertoires for as long as we can remember. Even as kids, before we could even come close to pronouncing this ungodly long word, we have manipulated others for the purpose of our own selfish needs.

Crazy & Obsessed
Addicted to Relationships

We pretend to cry and throw tantrums so our parents would buy us toys and pay attention to us.

We form cliques, selectively bribing those we want in our circles, for the purpose of building up our own reputations and finding reason to exclude those we dislike.

However, by doing this, we only hurt ourselves. We selectively deprive ourselves from the good that people have to offer us, and we write our own tragic endings. We obliviously train ourselves to believe that we know ourselves better than anyone else can know us, but in truth, we are the ones who know the least about ourselves even though we have the most potential to because we struggle to see ourselves outside of our relations to others.

Therefore, we attach quickly to our partners and significant others. When we are in a relationship, we sacrifice a huge part of ourselves to that other person, in a sense, we give ourselves to that other person, and they become the person who knows us best. So, when the relationship ends, we lose that part of ourselves and literally fall apart when they walk out of our lives.

Ultimately, so many of us become debilitated and depressed when we lose our partners. Every ounce of trust that we had put in that other person is now gone. The person we used to rely on to learn about ourselves and believe in ourselves is now gone.

Chapter Twelve

Mutual Breakups Are A Hoax

"As kids, we only shared when we expected something in return. As adults, we are not much different." ℒ

Mutual breakups, despite how much of a unanimous decision both parties say it is, are never mutual. There is no such thing as two people, who shared so much together, who can part ways without some sort of resentment, especially when one person moves on, and even more especially when one person moves on quickly.

Crazy & Obsessed
Addicted to Relationships

We begin to self-doubt and question all the things that went wrong, all our flaws, things we could have done better, and the reasons for our ex-partners choosing other people over us. Even if we know that the relationship was terrible and toxic for us, we place blame on ourselves because, when someone chooses not to be in our lives and chooses to be in someone else's instead, we start to believe that there is something inherently wrong with us, and we begin to dwell on our mistakes.

There is a saying I heard recently on the Internet, no surprise there, that when someone chooses to leave us or cheat on us when we have not already done the same, it reflects who THEY are, NOT who WE are. When people leave or cheat on decent partners, they are leaving and cheating themselves out of the good and happiness that come with having partners who care about them and are willing to do anything for them.

Remember, people leave and cheat because of their feelings AT THE TIME, not necessarily because of the situation or something that we did. People walk away from good partners because they selfishly expect more and believe they deserve more. Casting people aside to chase that rollercoaster dream of deservingness is never the answer.

Chapter Thirteen

The Broken Heart

"The heart can only be taken away when we relinquish ourselves to others. If we never expose ourselves, we will never be broken; however, we will also never learn to become whole." ℒ

I once dated someone who left me out of the blue because he said he feared commitment. This was the breakup that made me question my entire existence (I know, a little dramatic on my end), and made me hate myself and the world for months, only to find out that THIS SAME

Crazy & Obsessed
Addicted to Relationships

PERSON BETROTHED two months later. Fear of commitment, my ass!

I used to reflect on what his action said about me, but now I know that this reflects who THAT person was. Whether he lied or had been cheating on me the entire time we were together, all this did was show me how shitty other people can really be, and how we should not look at their actions as a reflection of our own humanities. I still believe that person had a good heart and is still one of the most amazing people I have ever met, but his actions reflected issues and problems that manifested in his own life, something that was outside of my knowledge and control.

People without trust and attachment issues do not get married after two months of knowing someone unless they are:

Actively trying to avoid turning back to their exes,

Actively trying to forget and distract themselves from past traumas,

Actively trying to commit to anyone they find because they are desperate to find "love,"

Actively trying to hurt someone,

Actively trying to uphold an image or,

Literally has such low self-esteem and self-worth that they would cheat themselves from the chance of getting to know someone before settling.

Crazy & Obsessed
Addicted to Relationships

We do not cheat on people or date multiple people at once unless we are searching for something within ourselves vicariously through other partners. We are not satisfied with how we feel about ourselves, and we do not feel fulfilled in our own lives, so we believe we can find ourselves in others.

We bounce from person to person because we falsely believe that there is someone out there who can make us feel whole about ourselves, who can give us the desires and needs we have dreamt about, who have unconditional acceptance of all our flaws and our nonsensical thoughts, and who can love us when it seems like no one else will ever love us again.

But that person is not someone we can meet on a dating app or in a bar.

That person is someone we come face to face with every day.

That person is someone who has been by our sides since the day we were born.

That person is our family, our friend, our confidant, and our partner through thick and thin.

That person is us.

Despite how hard we search and how many partners we go through, we will never find the person we truly are looking for until we have accepted the fact that we, ourselves, are the only ones who can complete us. All this endless searching and sleeping around only distract us from loving and accepting ourselves.

Crazy & Obsessed
Addicted to Relationships

We fight against ourselves because we are terrified of not being able to rely on something we can see with our eyes that is not a reflection. We do not trust ourselves because we do not love ourselves.

It is far easier to love something else or someone else because we can choose to only love the good and fake blind to the ugly. But with ourselves, we are forced to accept our flaws, flaws that we do not want to acknowledge are there, flaws that make us question why anyone would ever love us, and flaws that make us run from reality.

How can we turn the culture we live in from a culture of self-doubt, self-hate, and shame to a culture of self-acceptance and self-love, and see flaws as a part of existence and uniqueness rather than reasons to cast someone aside?

How can we stop selecting partners and friends based on external beauty and wealth, and focus on internal beauty and personality?

How can we learn to be happy for someone else's success rather than secretly hating them and cursing at them silently, hoping failure will soon fall upon them?

How can we learn to love, not only in a romantic way, but in an accepting way?

Chapter Fourteen

Get Over It Already

"Holding onto the past only makes it easier to forget about the present." ℒ

We all know the pattern.

Boy meets girl.

Boy and girl fall in love.

Boy and girl break up.

Crazy & Obsessed
Addicted to Relationships

Boy and girl avoid each other like a plague.

Boy and girl post Instagram pictures of their new catch to make each other jealous.

This is nothing new.

We all do this.

We all know people who do this.

We all pretend that we can walk away from romantic love as civil and mature people, but who are we kidding? The adults in us try to reason that our exes were not the right ones for us and that there are others far more suiting. The children in us think that our exes were assholes, that there is something wrong with us, and that we must stalk our exes and their new partners to find out why they chose them over us.

Naturally, our "id" forces us to behave in more childlike states and overpowers the "ego." Age does not play a role in which side we act more on. Whether we are 20 or 60, when we feel hurt, our raw emotions unleash, overtaking our logic, and we become the people that we judge.

How is it that, despite the numerous times we try to reason that our exes were not right for us, or that they just want different things at this point in time, we still fault ourselves? Whenever our hearts feel broken or betrayed, we revert to our adolescent states, where we religiously believe that the only possible reason that people do not want us is because we are not good enough as lovers or as people, and that we are flawed and unworthy of any connections. We let our emotions hurt us and turn us into a statistic.

Saying that we should stop letting breakups or divorces tear apart our lives is much easier than living that to fruition. It has been shown that when people emotionally feel a broken heart, their hearts LITERALLY BREAK. This is known as "Broken Heart Syndrome," and its symptoms mimic that of an actual heart attack.

When we feel hurt from separation, we experience immense stress in our hearts, chest pains, and shortness of breath. Therefore, many of us feel like we are unable to breathe when someone we love leaves us.

Contrary to what our friends and family say, this feeling is not an exaggeration. We are not being dramatic. The feeling is REAL. The pain is real and unless someone has experienced this first-hand, he/she will always continue to believe that we can just "heal" and "get over it." When we experience this, we believe that the ONLY person who can help us is the person who walked away from us.

We stalk, beg, and threaten suicide not because we are psychologically sick and disturbed, but because we are trying to HEAL OURSELVES. What our exes and bystanders see as us being "psychotic" are our broken hearts and minds attempting to heal.

Believe it or not, stalking is MEDICINE!

Begging is THERAPY!

It sounds insane to someone not going through it, but to those who are in it or have been through it, these

Crazy & Obsessed
Addicted to Relationships

behaviors are completely normal and justified. These crazy attempts we engage in to win someone back are our minds' attempts to heal our bodies from the physical pain we find unbearable.

Even when we know that the people we chase are not good for us, we chase after them anyway because we perceive these people as the only ones who can relieve our sufferings at the time.

These people do not even have to be alive. It is the ACTION of actively trying to win someone back that gives us the relief.

Similar to how addicts feel the rush from the ACT OF OBTAINING drugs rather than having the actual drugs, we feel the rush from knowing that we are taking the steps toward getting someone back despite whether we actually succeed.

We find satisfaction in mapping out our daily routes so we can "accidentally" run into our exes.

We find joy in writing out long and elaborate love letters, dreaming about how these letters are the perfect weapon in making our exes fall in love with us again.

We bask in the idea of what it would feel like to reunite with someone rather than the actual reunion.

How many of you have ever spent months trying to win someone back, but when that person does come back and want to be with you, you no longer want them?

I have.

Crazy & Obsessed
Addicted to Relationships

This is because we are addicted to the chase.

The chase is our medicine.

We expend all our efforts on the JOURNEY that, when the destination finally arrives, we are already relieved from the physical pain and no longer want anything to do with our exes.

So, what is the lesson here?

To the victims of our crazy behaviors, understand that we are only trying to heal ourselves, and we are not as psychotic as you may think.

To those we call "crazy," check in with yourself.

Is this a constant pattern in your life after the end of a relationship?

Is this how you really want to be portrayed?

In your mind, your crazy behaviors are justified.

In someone else's mind, you may be branded as the "crazy ex."

As much as we want people to understand that we are only messed up because we need to heal, mental medicine is still not as understandable as physical medicine.

Chapter Fifteen

You Are Crazy. Deal With It!

"I would rather be seen as "crazy" than be seen as "ordinary." ℒ

Be the crazy that you are.

Embrace the crazy that you have.

We are all crazy.

Hell, shout from the top of a building and EXPRESS YOUR CRAZINESS!

Crazy & Obsessed
Addicted to Relationships

There is NOTHING WRONG with SHARING our emotions, EXPRESSING our anger, and UNLEASHING the painful feelings that we so often keep hidden.

Unfortunately, we also do not want to risk losing ourselves and our self-respects, and we especially want to avoid letting those who hurt us take away our identities.

So, what is the solution?

Unleash all the craziness in private?

Stalk cardboard cutouts of our exes instead of the actual people?

Scream into a bag?

The truth is, there is no solution.

The very thing that provides immediate relief for our pain is also the very thing that can bring us to our own demise.

Do we risk appearing insane to allow our minds and souls to heal?

Do we maintain our sanities and succumb our hearts to internal damage?

Do we choose to protect ourselves from ourselves or choose to protect ourselves from others?

We all know the saying, "We are our own worst enemies." Suicide rates soar with each passing year. Every twelve minutes, someone commits suicide in the United States, with 120 suicides every day and close to 45,000 suicides every year. Knowing these statistics, ask yourself again, would you risk your mental health to protect your mental pride?

Would you hold in your life-threatening emotions to protect yourself from how the shallow and misunderstood world sees you?

At the end of the day, you are left alone with yourself.

Would you rather be left alone with the "you who accepts who you are," or would you rather be locked up alone with the "you who regrets the choices that you have made"?

Chapter Sixteen

Who The Hell Are You?!

"If you look in the mirror and do not recognize yourself, smash it, and unleash your inner soul." ℒ

Who are we outside of a relationship?

Are we just seen as people in relation to those around us?

Our mother's daughter.

Our husband's wife.

Crazy & Obsessed
Addicted to Relationships

Our child's mother.

Are we just seen as important due to our labels?

A writer.

An actress.

A motivational speaker.

Can we ever be someone of value without an association?

We live in a world where being alone is "pathetic," and we are taught to be ashamed of it.

Because of this, we have become afraid of being lonely and would rather settle for abusive relationships.

We form partnerships with people we cannot stand just so we can tell others that we have someone significant in our lives.

We blatantly ignore the people we are with 364 days of the year so we can find a reason to celebrate Valentine's Day.

We plaster our "happiness" and "love" all over social media to give others the illusion of our newly formed connections and lack of loneliness, when in reality, we are dying from internal loneliness.

Internal loneliness does not stem from physical loneliness. Internal loneliness stems from the lack of satisfaction with ourselves.

Crazy & Obsessed
Addicted to Relationships

Even when we are surrounded by people, we can still feel alone.

When we are not satisfied with ourselves, our lives, and the choices we make, what we have and who we are with have no meaning. We can lie to others by pretending to be happy, but we can never lie to ourselves. Many have tried, zero have succeeded. Even if we do plaster on that fake smile every day and tell ourselves that our lives are good, our minds and hearts know the truth. If we are not happy with the choices we have made, our bodies will tell us.

Depression will kick in.

Anxiety will creep up.

We will catapult from being fine one minute to having a mental breakdown the next.

We will always be lonely if we remain dishonest with ourselves.

Infinite number of Instagram followers and Facebook friends mean nothing if we are not friends with ourselves.

We can walk away from friends, relationships, people we find incredibly intolerable, family, colleagues, even our religions, but we cannot walk away from ourselves.

Even if we change our identities and develop an entirely new personality, we will still be forced to deal with the guilt and shame of doing so, eventually developing a fear or intense hatred toward our new selves.

Crazy & Obsessed
Addicted to Relationships

The only way to truly run away from ourselves is death.

Learning to love ourselves is one of the hardest things we have to do in life, as silly as it may seem. But this is something that we must learn to do if we ever want to stop running.

I ran from myself for years, turning to addictions to distract myself from myself.

I ran across the world to try to get away from my own thoughts of self-hatred and denial.

Running only makes it worse.

Running only delays the process of healing and self-acceptance.

Running builds upon the shit that we are already facing.

Would you rather deal with one piece of shit now or deal with piles of shit later?

We cannot run.

We cannot hide.

Stand up.

Look in the mirror.

Acknowledge that you exist.

Smile.

Crazy & Obsessed
Addicted to Relationships

Tell yourself that you deserve to be okay.

Tell yourself that you deserve to be loved.

Chapter Seventeen

Stranger Danger

"The stranger sitting across from you, winking at you while you avoid eye contact, can very well be your next spouse." ℒ

Just as abuse from a loved one can cause us to shut ourselves out from our friends and family, abuse from a stranger can also have the same effect. At least 80% of the world participate in some sort of dating app, whether it is Tinder, OkCupid, POF, Match, you name it. We all know that being hurt by loved ones can tear our souls apart. However, being hurt by strangers can also leave us incapacitated.

A stranger can walk into our lives, change everything for the better, and then walk out just as quickly as they came in.

A stranger can walk into our lives, destroy us, decide to stay, AND WE LET THEM!

Earlier, I had mentioned how short-term relationships can hurt just as equally, if not more, than long-term relationships due to how we only see "perfection" in short-term partners rather than the flaws they hide from us.

However, imagine meeting the perfect person, infinite common interests, nonstop sparks, pretty much the person of your dreams one minute, and the next, they give you the cold shoulder, tell you that they do not want a relationship, that they do not want you, or even worse, that they are already taken.

Crushed, right???

You become devastated and overwhelmed with so much pain and agony that you either attempt to convince that person to love you, like a crazy person, or you give up on love and vow to die alone. As dramatic and immature as this may seem, we know EXACTLY how this feels, regardless of age and life-experiences.

Human beings are fragile and our emotions tend to override who we are as people. In cases of love and romantic relationships, we turn to extremes. We either completely shut off our emotions, for the fear of further experiencing pain and heartbreak, or we allow our emotions to become vulnerable. We are often told that when it comes to romantic companions, we need to use our common sense and give when we need to give, but also hold back when giving becomes too much. However, this is more viable in theory than in reality.

Love is a drug and, many times, we cannot control how we behave when it comes to love. The phrase "head over heels" exists because, when we fall, we fall hard. This is especially the case for those who feel lonely and still affected by the betrayal of previous endeavors.

Loneliness and pain drive us to use our hearts rather than our heads because, similar to drugs, the craving overpowers the logic. This makes us vulnerable to the manipulation of strangers we meet. We fall for strangers quickly because they represent freedom from loneliness and freedom from pain. We channel our vulnerable emotions toward people we do not know for two reasons:

Emotional support from strangers comes with the benefit of non-judgments because they do not know who we are or where we have come from and,

Strangers provide distraction from the current bullshit in our lives and distraction from having to face the reality of living with ourselves.

What does this all lead to?

Abuse.

From strangers.

Crazy & Obsessed
Addicted to Relationships

Disgust.

For ourselves.

At one point or another in our lives, most of us have allowed strangers to take advantage of us when we were at our worst, ranging from going on dates with people we did not find attractive to one-night stands and sexual assaults. Looking back, from the logical standpoint, we know the stupidity that comes with allowing strangers to take advantage of us. We blame ourselves because, on some level, we were probably too distraught and sad to remember that we gave consent to our Tinder dates to take our pants off.

This is a clear difference from rape, unfortunately. When we are sober but still fail to tell the other person to stop, or when we freeze up when someone is trying to have sex with us, allowing it to happen, we can no longer consider this rape. We can become so emotionally vulnerable that a single human touch can drive away our logical thoughts.

How many of you have ever felt numb or regret DURING sex but FAILED to say anything to stop it and instead, closed your eyes and prayed that it was OVER soon?

This is the work of our emotions. When we do not know what we want and when our emotions become overwhelming, we freeze, and we become paralyzed. We lose our words, and we pray the night away, pushing off the consequences until the next day.

So, how do we stop these overwhelming feelings and numbness?

Crazy & Obsessed
Addicted to Relationships

How do we stop letting strangers take advantage of us?

How do we stop relinquishing our power and control to those who abuse them?

Even though it is easier said than done, we MUST acknowledge before going into any kind of situation with strangers whether we are going into it because we ACTUALLY like them or because we feel LONELY and HEARTBROKEN. I struggle with this all the time, and I still struggle with this. I let my anger from seeing an ex, or someone I once loved, with someone else turn into meaningless sex with the first person interested in me. I realize why I do this, and I realize the consequences from doing this, but I still do it anyway.

Anger and jealousy are some of the most difficult emotions to overcome. Similarly, when we are starving, we will eat anything, and we will take all the necessary actions to do so until we are full. These are called the "Deadly Sins" for a reason. They drive us toward one goal, stopping only when we have achieved it, regardless of what and who we destroy along the way.

Chapter Eighteen

Societal Rules Shall Die

"Our lives are not based on reality; our lives are based on what we perceive as reality." ℒ

We grew up in a society where the idea of a relationship is commonly related to the idea of sacrificing our own lives for the benefit of someone else's, where we must give up our one chance for happiness to make someone else happy.

Wait.

Crazy & Obsessed
Addicted to Relationships

WHAT??!?!

Who the hell decided that this was the standard to live by?

Better yet, who the hell decided to follow these rules?!?

The phrases "happy wife, happy life" and "life ends with marriage" are two of the most nonsensical phrases that people have chosen to use as their mantras. Although we most often associate these phrases with men who give up their freedom and souls for women, women also often give up their lives for the sake of relationships. Men and women equally give up their dreams, their family, their friends, their hobbies, and even their careers for relationships and marriages.

When we fall in love, we make sacrifices so that others will stay and continue to love us. We give and give to other people, catering to their needs, such as giving up friends of the opposite sex to avoid relationship conflicts or giving up our homes to move across the country for our partners' job relocations, until we have nothing left to give.

Why should we give up our chances at happy lives to support our spouses who, keep in mind, are full-grown adults?

Or, why are we not able to support them and STILL live our own lives?

I believe that the reason we hold to heart these beliefs of one-way sacrifices is because we fall for people who only look out for themselves, people who take from us until we have nothing left so we must abide by their demands. We become so afraid of losing these people that we convince ourselves to give up our chances at happiness because, if these people are happy, then we are "happy."

Our friends and family tell us that we deserve better, but we do not say anything nor do we acknowledge them because we have already fallen for the trap of loving people who do not love us back.

We have this list of what it means to find the "perfect" partner, and we are willing to give up true love for the image of being with someone "perfect." Stop holding onto expectations that we MUST be with someone wealthy and beautiful in order to have a happy life and a happy marriage.

We live in the 21st Century! We do not need some white-collared pimp to take care of us because we are independent and successful human beings who can take care of ourselves, and we do not need to have beautiful babies with Victoria Secret models because beauty is subjective!

JUST.

STOP.

Everyone is beautiful, and everyone deserves a chance at life. The term "ugly baby" is sickening because those who truly think that babies can be ugly, that innocent and helpless infants can be disgusting, should be punched in the face. We need to fall in love with and marry those who will be by our sides no matter what.

Crazy & Obsessed
Addicted to Relationships

What happens when we lose our jobs and stop bringing home luxurious gifts every night?

What happens when we lose our muscles and replace them with fat?

Will our partners leave us because we are no longer rich and fit?

Should we even give a shit if our disgustingly shallow partners leave us?

We are worth so much more than our paychecks and our looks!

If our partners decide to leave us for someone wealthier or prettier, will we still be able to look at ourselves in the mirror at the end of the day?

We need to know that we are worth loving just as we are, not because we are rich, smart, pretty, or whatever other "positive" terms that people seem to value.

We need to stop trying to impress people who walk in and out of our lives quicker than we can say "fucked up."

When we let the values of others define who we are, we lose ourselves.

We are not defined by others, and our lives should not be put in their hands.

What makes them more deserving than us?

Crazy & Obsessed
Addicted to Relationships

What gives them the power to dictate whether we move on or lie deep in depression?

We need to find partners who love us for everything we are: crazy, stupid, the face we are without a pound of makeup, the value we are worth if we lose our jobs, and everything else in between.

We need to find partners who support us to be the best that WE can be, not the best that they want us to be.

We need to find partners who, despite all obstacles, will always find a way to make the relationships work.

We need to stop the endless patterns of infidelity and divorce by choosing people who care for us, not people we HOPE can care for us.

When we are forced to try even a little, and I mean a micro amount, to get others to love us and want to be with us, they are no longer worth the effort.

Love is not something we need to chase after.

Love is something that finds us.

Having partners who truly love us means having partners who will NEVER make us work for them.

Human beings are not meant to chase after one another. We are not supposed to subject ourselves to that level of worthlessness, where we allow other human beings to treat us as less deserving.

Crazy & Obsessed
Addicted to Relationships

I do not give a fuck how rich, how hot, or how Ryan Gosling this other person is; no man or woman is worth CHASING after, and no man or woman is worth our submission.

We need to stop being afraid of ending up alone, and we need to stop giving people chances they do not deserve because we are afraid of losing them. When we find the right people, the people who are MEANT to be in our lives, not the people we WANT in our lives, we TAKE our lives back. We GAIN ourselves back because we REPLACE toxicity with the support of those who genuinely want to see us succeed.

Until then, do not be afraid of waiting. Stop pouting and bitching about how you are going to end up alone when you are only 30. The average age of millennials getting married is 35, but even then, so what?

Why rush into marriage if it is just going to add more stress, burden, and pain to the hardships that already exist?

What is the benefit of marrying someone who is completely wrong for us and raising a family for reason of status?

Nothing!

It is much less anxiety provoking to WAIT and LIVE our lives the way we WANT than endure years of pain and suffering just to end up in divorce, or even worse, in marriages that make us want to jump out a window. When we stop being so afraid of living on our own, when we stop trying to search for love via ten different dating apps and start finding love within, we start realizing that others are only added bonuses to what we already possess, not sole necessities. The purpose of finding a partner is to share with someone the happiness that we already have in our own lives, not to achieve happiness.

When we start respecting others more than we respect ourselves, we need to hop on a plane, go live on a mountain, and figure out what the fuck went wrong with our sense of logic.

Okay, maybe not to that extreme, but we do need to force ourselves to have a reality check and realize that we are worth so much more than our labels as "belongings." We are not labeled as "someone's spouse"; we are labeled as "I."

We are NOBODY WITHOUT OURSELVES!

Stop trying to find purpose through others and learn to find purpose WITHIN.

Being ALIVE, even if we are alone, is enough to be meaningful in this world.

STOP taking shit from those who think they are more valuable than we are!

Chapter Nineteen

Seriously, We Do Not Know What The Fuck We Want

"Those who have everything are those who feel lost in emptiness." ℒ

We tell ourselves that we just want to love.

We tell ourselves that we just want to find someone kind and honest who will love us back.

We fantasize about finding a partner who is patient, understanding, and accepting of all that we are.

Crazy & Obsessed
Addicted to Relationships

So, why do we deceive ourselves into accepting anything less than that?

We are so afraid of being alone that we settle way too much, and we would rather be miserable than alone at the age of 30. How often do we hear horror stories of couples divorcing, especially those who anointed their marriages in their 20s? Our fears overpower our abilities to see beyond the consequences of present moments. We cannot logically see past our immediate fears and into future consequences, in that, marrying people we do not love will only end in misery and migraines.

We let our emotionally-charged selves and our irrational fears dictate our love lives and force us to "love" the first person willing to love us back. We deceive ourselves into believing that we are truly in love because we become so paranoid that if we do not marry the person who somewhat tolerates our flaws, then we will never find someone who will.

How many times have you walked out of a relationship and back into the dating scene, just to reminisce about your ex and how much you miss him/her?

When we have a FEW bad experiences with a FEW new people, we either want to give up on love completely, or we turn back to our exes because of the familiarity. Dramatic, right?

GROW A PAIR!

We have the tendency to turn back to our pasts, not necessarily because we love them, but because with time, we forget their flaws and zoom in on their positive qualities, qualities that made us fall for them in the first place, rather than qualities that made us walk out.

We tell ourselves, "Our exes were sweet, loving, generous, funny, and patient," but we forget to tell ourselves that our exes were also abusive, unfaithful, deceitful, lazy, and manipulative.

We ignore the reasons for our previous relationships ending and revert to them when we fail to make other connections within a month or two of dating. 99% of the time, this does not mean that we want to be with our exes; we may still love them, and we may always love them because they were a huge presence in our lives, but we may not actually want to be with them. We only think we do because we lack the patience to wait for our next partners.

Dating shortly after a breakup usually ends in a disaster. We compare new people to the old, and we set the bar so high that we deprive new potential partners of any chance if they do not meet the EXACT qualities that we are looking for. We also date with hopes that the next person we meet is the person we marry.

When that does not go as planned, and most of the time it does not, we attempt to rekindle relationships from our pasts, believing that we may have made a mistake in letting our potential spouses leave.

We hate waiting. We would much rather jump from person to person, from relationship to relationship, than deal with being single for more than a couple of months.

We HATE the idea of being SINGLE.

Crazy & Obsessed
Addicted to Relationships

When we are single in our mid-20s to early-40s, while the rest of our friends are married with kids, we feel like losers.

We feel like no one will ever want to be with us if they have not already by now.

We believe that we are unlovable and too crazy to be with.

We begin to hate couples, relationships, and all things related to love.

We do endless research on statistics of failed relationships and annoy everyone with that information.

We become miserable, and we want everyone around us to be miserable as well.

Why do we do this?

Why do we become anti-love venoms when we feel like we are the only ones alone?

We associate relationships as hallmarks of personal success and happiness.

False.

Relationships only serve to ENHANCE our personal success and happiness.

WE are the HALLMARKS of our own personal success and happiness.

Crazy & Obsessed
Addicted to Relationships

We struggle to acknowledge how much power we have because, ever since we were kids, we have been told that we should aim to find a wife/husband who can make us happy, start a family, and have kids so they can carry on our legacies. Some people spend their entire lives dedicated solely to finding their spouses.

Imagine this:

One chance in life.

One goal.

Find a spouse.

Sole dedication.

Lifetime of misery.

Never-ending.

Death.

Sounds pretty terrible, right?

Unfortunately, some people are STILL okay with that. They still believe that finding the "perfect" person is the ULTIMATE GOAL in life.

We are strong and capable of so much.

Why dedicate all that POTENTIAL to another person?

We have the skills of climbing Mount Everest,

Crazy & Obsessed
Addicted to Relationships

Winning Olympic medals,

Running with bulls,

Traveling around the world,

Creating artificial intelligence,

Building empires out of nothing,

Hiking across entire countries,

And SO MUCH MORE!

We have been able to ACCOMPLISH these goals on our OWN for decades because we never needed a partner by our sides to prove our strength and motivation!

So why do we need one now!?

That was a rhetorical question.

Do not answer it.

Seriously, shut up.

Take a lesson from those who are single AND happy. These are not people who are against relationships because they are anti-commitment.

These are people who ENJOY being with themselves rather than running away from themselves.

Crazy & Obsessed
Addicted to Relationships

These are people who do not rush from relationship to relationship because they know that finding someone who is not right for them will only end in self-destruction.

These are people who enjoy their own companies.

Instead of calling themselves "losers" for being single, they acknowledge that even though they are not in the company of another person, they can still enjoy life independently.

We all must learn how to live outside of a relationship. We may feel alone without a romantic partner, but we are never truly alone. We have friends, family, colleagues, pets and, most importantly, ourselves, to lift our spirits and support us when we have fallen.

Even if we are dating or in a relationship, we can still be alone. We cannot stick like glue to our partners forever. People have their own activities and commitments and sometimes, believe it or not, they DO NOT involve us.

We cannot follow someone 24/7 because we will look PSYCHOTIC if we do. We cannot sit around, do nothing, and wait for someone to come back because we will look PATHETIC. We are already learning how to be alone when we are IN a relationship, so let us channel that to when we are NOT in a relationship?

Is it because we miss having someone to rely on and communicate with daily?

We can still have that!

Crazy & Obsessed
Addicted to Relationships

Pick up the phone and call your parents once in a while! You know they need it!

Is it because we miss having someone to talk to and trust? Friends are called "friends" for a reason, and if they are truly our friends, they will be the "hand of trust" for us regardless of how busy they are. However, friends can also sit in the grey area. If our friends are too "busy" for us or too "in a relationship" for us, then they were never truly our friends. There are billions of people in this world with kind and decent hearts who will jump over lava to offer a helping hand. Shitty friends can be replaced.

Is it because we miss the feeling of human touch and affection?

Although this is much more difficult to find when we are single, we can still provide affection for ourselves.

Why not give yourself a hug?

You may look stupid while doing it, but why not try hugging yourself once or twice a day, and saying "I love you" in the mirror?

It can be an eye-opening experience to know that we can physically and emotionally love ourselves.

If that is not enough, get a dog.

Dogs will give us more affection than we will ever want, and better yet, without strings attached.

Crazy & Obsessed
Addicted to Relationships

We do not have to make promises to dogs or buy them anything to receive affection. Dogs will give us affection even when we are mad at them.

Dogs are fucking amazing.

Get a dog.

Okay, so we know about the people who serially enter new relationships to avoid being alone, but what about the flip side? What about the people who never want to be in relationships and only serially date, going from one person to the next after 1-2 dates? Whether this applies to us or someone we know, when someone is so resistant to enter a relationship, they tend to use these common excuses (hint: watch for red flags!):

"I am too busy to dedicate time to a relationship."

"I get bored when I spend too much time with one person."

"I do not like commitments because I tend to flake on them."

"My family takes up all my time."

Here is my personal favorite:

"I am not relationship material."

Fuck you too, dude!

While there are SOME truths to these excuses, they all stem from one internal reason: FEAR.

Crazy & Obsessed
Addicted to Relationships

The fear of being hurt or the fear of hurting.

Let us first explore the fear of being hurt, which has already been touched upon earlier.

Whatever the reason, past trauma, paranoia, or indirect experiences from relationships with others, we all have deep fears of getting hurt, refusing to give others the power to control our feelings. We become overly independent, not because we love ourselves, but because we know that we can CONTROL ourselves. We trust no one because anyone can have the motive and desire to hurt us.

When we take trust away from others, family included, we prevent ourselves from getting burned. However, we also devoid ourselves from the love that comes from trusting someone else. Nothing is a necessity in life, relationships included, and we can choose to have one or not. But there is also a difference between wanting to be alone and not serially dating versus wanting to be alone and serially dating.

When we serially date and never settle, we crave the feeling of being with someone, but we still fear getting hurt, so once we start feeling a sense of commitment, we bail. When we serially date, we are not okay with being alone. We want to be with someone, but we do not allow ourselves to do so.

On the flip side, sometimes we resist entering new relationships because we fear hurting others. We may still be hung up on those from our pasts, or we are too afraid to let those we are not interested in down, aka the creation of "ghosting." We continue seeing people we do not see futures with while also dating others because we are too afraid to let anyone down.

Regardless of the reason, when we make an effort to avoid hurting even just one person, we end up hurting everyone, including ourselves.

Chapter Twenty

Taking Our Lives Back

"Carve your own future by fighting for your present. The winner shall be deemed victorious of your life." ℒ

I want to stress how important it is to take a breather when you feel like your face is about to explode.

Breathe in.

Pause.

Breathe Out.

Crazy & Obsessed
Addicted to Relationships

Pause.

Repeat.

When we find ourselves excessively texting and calling someone who wants nothing to do with us, we are only hurting ourselves.

When we find ourselves obsessively thinking about someone who refuses to love us, we are only delaying the time it takes for us to move on.

When people refuse to be in our lives, nothing in the world will make them change their minds unless THEY want to change their minds.

Contacting them nonstop will NOT make them want to answer us.

Camping outside their front doors will only make them call the cops.

Serenading them from the top of a building, surrounded by doves, will only force them to turn the other way.

We can be as loving, as affectionate, as compassionate, and as passionate as we want, but when someone wants to ignore us, we are GOING TO BE IGNORED!

I have been kicked and slapped (by myself) in the face for continuing to obsess over people not worth obsessing over. I keep trying to remind myself that if Mr. Loser and Sir Unavailable still wanted to be with me, they would. They have my number. They know where to find me.

Crazy & Obsessed
Addicted to Relationships

BUT THEY DO NOT COME!

BECAUSE THEY DO NOT FUCKING CARE!

AND NEITHER SHOULD I!

NEITHER SHOULD WE!

We are all INTELLIGENT people who know DAMN WELL that we should not waste our time on toxic people, but WE DO IT ANYWAY. The romantic side of us continue to hold onto the hope that one day the ones we loved will come back.

We dream about this.

We lose sleep over this.

This idea consumes our minds day and night because we once had something amazing who are now strangers.
We pray that they will still come running back.

Unfortunately, people usually only run back to us in movies. In real life, people leave, and they just leave. There is no regret, no compassion, and no sorrow. They know we are suffering, and they thrive on it. Even the most selfless people can become cold and selfish when people refuse to accept their decisions.

We need to stop losing our values and dignities over unrequited love.

We need to forgive those who hurt us and move on.

Crazy & Obsessed
Addicted to Relationships

Even if we still love them, letting go is the most loving and selfless act we can do.

If we wanted to leave, and someone was incessantly trying to hold us back, we would become angry and distant also.

Let them go.

They might come back.

They might not.

That is an inevitable risk that we must take if we want to stop being depressed and learn to love again.

Holding onto false hope only makes us feel worse.
Sure, sending that text and waiting optimistically for them to maybe respond can be uplifting and thrilling in the moment.

But what happens when they do not respond?

Our hearts sink.

We react toward their silence by continuing to send messages, and we eventually spiral out of control, leaving us feeling worse than before.

This is how patterns form.

We like to believe that one innocent, "how are you?" can do no harm, but that one innocent text soon becomes, "I fucking hate you for ignoring me! Please answer me! Please come back to me! I love you, and I cannot live another day without you because every minute without you makes me miserable, and I am so depressed that I cannot focus on life anymore!"

It is CRAZY how that switch can happen within a time span of ten minutes, but we all know how familiar this sounds and how often we use variations of these same exact words. BEGGING is NOT attractive, and it further PUSHES people away.

However, if there is still a sliver of hope that begging can cause people to have a change of heart, we grab onto that hope and act on it. Soon, it becomes comfortable to beg, plead, and cry until we are left rotting in our torn pajamas and trash-filled apartment for months.

No one can love us if we do not have self-respect and self-love.

Chapter Twenty-One

We Can Heal

"The words 'can' and 'cannot' are only words; they only take form of the meanings we provide to them." ℒ

We can all heal because we are all victims despite our roles in breakups.

We all get hurt.

Crazy & Obsessed
Addicted to Relationships

We all feel guilty.

We all have regrets.

We all have pain in our hearts.

We all need comfort and closure.

We all need people to confide in.

Most importantly, we all need to forgive so we can heal.

Forgive the ones who walk away from us.

Forgive the ones who tell us we are not worth staying loyal to.

Forgive the ones who drive us to our breaking points.

Forgive the ones who force us to walk away for our own sanities.

Forgive the ones who deceive us into forming relationships with them.

Forgive the ones who betray our trusts.

Forgive the ones who cheat on us.

Forgive everyone who has ever hurt us and let go of grudges.

While it may seem therapeutic to hate those who hurt us and swear to never have anything to do with them again, when we continue to hate people with such passion long

Crazy & Obsessed
Addicted to Relationships

after heartbreak, it is because we hate ourselves. Most of us do not love ourselves enough to stop our hateful thinking. We falsely believe that we love ourselves so we do everything we can to have others also believe that we love ourselves. We join meditation retreats, take ourselves out on dates, and write "#iloveme!" on our mirrors to deceive ourselves into believing that we have self-love.

Do we though?

Our actions and thoughts when we are in our worst moments truly reflect how we think of ourselves.

We are not our hashtags.

We are far from who we present to the world.

It is okay to not love ourselves as much as we should.

It is okay to smile at the world while dying on the inside.

It is okay to feel negative emotions toward other people.

The only thing that is not okay is lying about it, pretending that we are happy and full of life when all we want to do is say "fuck you."

The guilt that comes from knowing that we are living a lie eventually tears us apart.

We can try to pretend that we are not living in a lie, but the truth will always be there.

Shoving it under a rug will only cause further detriment to ourselves.

Crazy & Obsessed
Addicted to Relationships

To self-love is to self-discover. We need to get to the core of who we are and what we are capable of before we can contribute to the lives of others. Think about it, how on earth are we supposed to dedicate our lives and time to other people when we, ourselves, are a mess? There is not enough of us to go around!

Other people are living, soulful creatures, just like us, and if we dive into their lives and interfere with their journeys when we are not prepared, we are only going to fuck them over even more, and that is not love. Unless we only want partners for the sake of manipulating and using them for our own benefits, without giving a damn about them, we cannot be with others until we can learn to love and accept being alone.

If we truly love the ones we claim to love, we would never want to do anything to hurt them, and by trying to be with them before we are ready to do so, we are actively beginning the journey toward their pain.

Even though the journey toward self-discovery is a never-ending path, we need to still reach the point where, if someone we love leaves us, we do not result in complete meltdowns, a feat that proves challenging for many.

We need to accept that we cannot force everyone to love us, that openly expressing love to someone does not always mean it will be returned, and that the only person we can count on to love us, is us.

Our own lives are the only ones we can control.

We cannot change love, and we cannot stop love from changing.

Crazy & Obsessed
Addicted to Relationships

When we choose to love, we choose to accept the pain that inevitably comes with it.

No relationship is without pain.

No marriage is without agony.

The difference between what keeps people together and what tears them apart is their resiliency as individuals, how capable they are at tackling and solving challenges that arise, and how willing they are to keep going despite all odds.

Such as those who can keep going and maintain a positive attitude after a relationship ends versus those who lock themselves away for days and turn to drugs and rebound sex as distractions.

None of us have it all figured out, not in life, not in relationships, not in family, and not in our careers. Most of us are only doing our best to survive and make it through each day while the rest of us reject these responsibilities and deny that they exist. I want to believe that we are all doing the best that we are capable of.

I want to believe that the reason life fails on us is because our best is just not good enough in some circumstances, which is okay, and not because some of us are too selfish and lackadaisical to put in the effort.

However, even with my naïve thinking, I know that most of us fall within the latter group. Because we have been taught to fend for ourselves and look out for our own happiness before anyone else's, we somehow translate that into self-absorption, resulting in taking from others rather than learning to give.

These are the people who use others to satisfy themselves.

These are the leeches who suck other people dry, draining them of their energy just to temporarily feel happier.

I am not innocent of this. I have used people, and I have also been used. We train our brains to become selfish, to take for self-survival, and to push down anyone who gets in our ways. We follow the norms and take all means necessary to reach conventional goals that we may or may not want.

Chapter Twenty-Two

My Obsession

"I cannot remember the exact moment when I became addicted to love. Perhaps I never will. All I know is that I am, and I cannot stop." ℒ

My obsession with men and the idea of "fantasy love" started when I was five. I sat next to this boy who I fantasized about spending my life with ever since he gave me a Christmas card featuring two teddy bears hugging each other. I thought this meant he was in love with me, whether he was or not, and I fell in love with him IMMEDIATELY.

This obsession lasted for the next eight years. I was a shy and timid child so I never had the nerve to say anything to him; I just avoided him as much as I could and spent those eight years journaling, in detail, about how we were going to spend the rest of our lives together.

To this day, I still do not know how he felt about me.

I wish I knew.

I wish I had said something.

Instead, every time he dated other girls, I psycho-stalked them, meticulously researching what they had that made them "better" than me.

Nothing!

Other than a little confidence and sluttiness.

Nothing!

During my sophomore year of high school, I somehow fell in love, yes somehow, with another boy whom I had turned down in middle school. I thought he was more disgusting than rotten cheese, and I made every effort to let him know that.

But, when he started dating and fucking someone other chick, someone whom I have hated since the day I met her because I thought she was trying to steal my personality, I felt the competition, and I suddenly wanted the man I had previously turned down.

I made every effort to be as platonic as possible, but when his girlfriend started seeing me as a threat for being his friend (I have known this kid since I was four!), she did everything she could, even threatened to self-harm, to get him to stop talking to me. And boy, did her methods work! He stopped talking to me.

GUESS WHAT?!

This drove me INSANE! So, I BECAME INSANE. I did everything I could to try to get him to speak to me, including creating a fake alias and lying about how I had Leukemia.

Yes, I am aware that my methods of trying to get someone to speak to me are a little unconventional.

Yes, I am also aware that I will never be the right person, in any way, shape, or form, to give anyone relationship advice.

Fast forward a couple of years, I start dating my first boyfriend, my first relationship that was not a fantasy. This relationship started off great, taking my mind off the mess that I had dealt with thus far, making me feel like I can be "normal" for a change.

That did not last long.

For some reason, reason even I could not understand, I deliberately tried to sabotage the relationship by bringing up problems that did not exist and stirred up jealousy at every corner I turned.

I did not want the relationship to end.

I just wanted the attention.

I craved the feeling of someone pining over me, chasing me, and expressing how much he cared about me, so much that I created drama just for that self-assurance.

I had such low self-esteem that I felt the need to destroy the emotions of others to build up my own.

I sought out arguments because I wanted more attention than what I was already getting.

I threw tantrums because I wanted someone to tell me that I was special when I was incapable of doing it myself.

Finally, it got to the point where he grew tired of all the drama I was creating and broke up with me...via text, taking us back to the synopsis shown at the very beginning of this book.

I repeat, I am not crazy.

Crazy actions do not make crazy people.

Crazy actions create emotional beings.

Between my first and second relationships, the whole three months, I wish I could say that I took time off for myself to recover and recuperate, the right way to deal with a difficult breakup.

Crazy & Obsessed
Addicted to Relationships

Instead, I found myself writing over 100 sappy love letters to my ex (AND ACTUALLY MAILING THEM!), flirting with as many people as I could find from over four different dating apps, and getting drunk/hooking up with random guys I had just met.

I was a mess.

I even hooked up with someone I met in a psychiatric ward, falling head-over-heels for him while also hating everything he was, writing a five-page love letter to him expressing how I felt, all after only knowing him for three weeks!!

I found myself "in love" with everyone who gave me the time of day, and I fantasized about my future with men after only the first date, including dates that did not even go well!

I was running away from myself.

I did not want to deal with the reality of my breakup.

I did not want to accept that it was over.

I could not get out of my own head.

The world felt like it revolved around me, and I could not objectively see how my actions were affecting others.

My second relationship did not stabilize my craziness as my first one did. In fact, it made it SO MUCH WORSE. I dove, head first, into my second relationship from day one, throwing myself at him sexually just to give him a reason to want to see me again.

Crazy & Obsessed
Addicted to Relationships

I have regretted it ever since.

However, at the time, I did not care.

I wanted someone to pay attention to me again.

I missed the feeling of constant love and affection.

I was going to do everything I could to get it.

Even if it meant abusing myself.

Unfortunately, my grand scheme of manipulation only works with pushovers, not those who have stubborn minds of their own. Acting the way that I had in my previous relationship only got me into a bigger mess than I had anticipated. After a month of dating, he broke up with me.

Naturally, I refused to accept that.

Let us keep in mind that I only knew this kid for a month, seeing each other twice a week, and I was already cyberstalking AND physically stalking him.

I even stalked and continuously messaged his FAMILY AND FRIENDS, trying to convince them to get him to talk to me after he HAD ALREADY BLOCKED ME.

When people block us, via phone AND social media, it is usually a sign that they want us gone.

Nope!

Crazy & Obsessed
Addicted to Relationships

I saw it as a motivator to try even harder to get his attention.

I skipped out on work early, just to take the bus to his apartment and knock on his door until he answered, because my anxiety took over.

I sent him gift and food deliveries with stupid little messages because I knew he would open his door for strangers when he did not open it for me.

That worked.

Once.

Until he stopped answering everyone altogether.

Fuck.

Long story short, I was able to get him to talk to me, and we eventually got back together…for three weeks, until he broke up with me again.

Of course, again, I refused to accept rejection so I pursued him.

This cycle became an on-and-off relationship with over 250 breakups!

Yes, I counted.

It was not love.

It was no longer my goal.

Crazy & Obsessed
Addicted to Relationships

It was miserable.

After a certain point, I did not even love him anymore. In fact, I do not even think I ever loved him in the first place!

I just loved the attention and the affection.

But I pursued.

And I stayed.

And I vowed, to both him and myself, to keep this relationship alive despite whatever happened.

He cheated on me.

I begged for forgiveness.

He hit me.

I justified that I deserved it.

He stole from me.

I looked the other way.

You are probably wondering the same thing that I had been: what the fuck is wrong with me?!

I could make up some sob story about fear and only staying because I was too afraid to be alone, but instead, I only stayed because...honestly, I have no idea why I stayed.

At the time, it just felt more comfortable staying, continuing to live in misery and pain, than leaving.

Day and night, I contemplated leaving. I imagined what life could be like with someone who respected me and did not abuse me. Then I think about how much effort I had put into getting my ex back, how shameful it would feel to throw it all away, and how much of a failure I would be if I could not hold onto a relationship even after sacrificing my self-respect.

I stayed with my abusive ex because, at the time, that pursuit was the only aspect in my life that I felt I could control. Somewhere in the mess of my on-and-off relationship, I had mentally shifted from obsessively being in "love" and obsessively wanting affection and attention to obsessively craving power.

You feel a certain sense of power when you can change a person's mind and manipulate situations so they are in your favor. Just like being in control of whether a relationship continues or ends gives power temporarily to one person over the other, being able to alter people's decisions and convince them to go against their original desires provides the same satisfaction.

We all want to feel powerful in at least one aspect of our lives whether it is in:

Relationships:

Through physical and emotional abuse

Making breadwinner choices

Engaging in temper tantrums and silent treatments when things do not go certain ways

Withholding pleasures until deeds are done

Jobs:

Snitching and stepping on the toes of others

Throwing coworkers under the bus to get ahead

Indulging in power trips

Our own bodies:

Constructing rigid diet and exercise plans to sculpt that "perfect" image of ourselves

Taking toxic diet pills and risking death just to stay thin

Throwing millions away on liposuction and plastic surgery

Power is fun. It gives us control over our lives when we feel we are losing it to others. But so many people get the wrong idea of what "control" really means. Control means taking BACK control of our OWN lives, NOT controlling the lives of OTHERS. We have this false perception that by controlling others and manipulating their feelings, we become in control of our own lives.

We believe "taking back power" means destroying the lives of others before they can destroy ours first.

Crazy & Obsessed
Addicted to Relationships

As much as we all want to believe that relationships are about equal amounts of love and respect, they are really about who has more control over the other. Think about it: ONE person always chooses the restaurant, ONE person always feels too "sick" to work, ONE person always decides on outings, and ONE person always chooses who the other can and cannot be friends with.

I am sure there are couples who do have equal balance in shared interests and opinions, but in most relationships, one person usually feels less in control and demeaned. Power and competition are inherent instincts that people possess.

We all want to feel strong.

No matter how hard we try to ignore this instinct, the moment we get the chance to order someone around and make that person bow down to our feet, we go for it.

Before I get carried away with my tangent, let me continue my story about my reckless cycle of obsession and insanity when it comes to men. After my seemingly never-ending breakup/makeup cycle with my second ex, the relationship FINALLY came to an end, to no one's surprise. And you know what? For the FIRST time, and probably the ONLY time in my series of dating adventures so far, I felt FREE and RELIEVED to not be in a relationship. I was HAPPY that he was no longer in my life. I did not even feel the need to TEXT HIM!

Of course, like the end of any kind of relationship, I still wondered about him, thought about him, and maybe occasionally stalked his Facebook five times a day, but remind you, I WAS RELIEVED and NOT AT ALL OBSESSED.

But habit is habit, right?

Can we really turn it off?

It is like breathing.

When we go too long without engaging in the habits that we have been used to for so long, we become strangers to ourselves.

Our usual behaviors now become nonexistent, and we are left experiencing an out-of-body feeling with our minds floating around, confused and lost.

The concrete schedule that we had of:

Texting every hour

Stalking every two hours

Nonstop Google searches of "How to Win Back Your Ex"

Constant thoughts of "Is he seeing someone else?"

Piles of books on "How Can I Get Him to Pay Attention to Me?" and

Endless nightmares of "How the FUCK can he be dating SOMEONE ELSE ALREADY?!"

Crazy & Obsessed
Addicted to Relationships

When my previous relationships ended, I obsessed over these thoughts and resources constantly. I did not want to move on, and I could not get over the breakups. I meticulously researched every book and every blog on how to win back exes and how to manipulate them into getting back together with me. I tried everything, from constant texting so they would not forget about me to not texting at all as per the dumb "No Contact Rule."

I wrote love letters, pouring my heart out in every metaphor and poem I could think of, begged for forgiveness and made false promises to change when I had no intention to, and sent hate messages to every girl who commented on their pages (despite whether they were family).

I did not care.

You might think that by doing all this, I had already lost myself, lost sight of the independent person I was born to be and turned into an obsessive monster who spent hours Googling biased blog posts on "How to Win Him Back When He No Longer Wants You."

I could literally take all the resources I found, slap them together, and create an entire library on this one topic alone.

I was very invested.

However, I did not lose myself.

Because I never knew who I was in the first place.

Crazy & Obsessed
Addicted to Relationships

So, by doing this, I was at least able to throw myself into a scenario where I felt both grounded and distracted from the spirals inside my head.

However, this was much more than just a surface desire, much more than just a "I need a distraction," a "I want him back," or a "I need to fuck someone new and move on."

This was about my struggles.

My demons.

My insecurities.

My desperate need to break something that was already broken.

When people end relationships, they grieve, they hate, but then they move on.

I struggled with that.

Instead, I begged, threatened suicide, threw tantrums, manipulated, ruined the lives of innocent people, and got myself into dangerous situations because "if it is not sketchy AF, then it is not enough of a distraction."

What is wrong with me?

No, really?

Why do I put myself through situations where it is literally life or death?

Crazy & Obsessed
Addicted to Relationships

Why do I put myself in scenarios where I feel so out of touch with myself, and I only begin to feel a sense of satisfaction AFTER I have latched myself onto someone I do not even know?

I fall "in love" with the first boy who winks at me.
IN LOVE!?!!!

My self-esteem is so low that I am willing to settle and love literally anyone who walks by me.

A random boy waves, my heart sinks.

Someone smiles at me; I dream of a fairytale wedding with him.

I struggle with distinguishing between feeling love and feeling infatuation.

I cannot separate how I ACTUALLY feel from how I WANT to feel.

Is this a problem that only I seem to have, where I believe every first date automatically warrants into a relationship?

Am I the only one who thinks I am actually FALLING IN LOVE after ONE DATE?

I mean, I know I am not actually falling in love, but it feels like it when we become so desperate to be with someone.

We see happy couples all around us.

Crazy & Obsessed
Addicted to Relationships

We hear our family and friends criticize how we are still single at 30, making us just want to snag a beau of our own to shut them all up!

So, am I crazy?

Or have the influences that surrounded me turned me into the monster I am today?

Chapter Twenty-Three

Stop Judging Us Based On Our Pasts!

"We all have scars, visible or not. Take your eyes off mine and focus on your own." ℒ

Sigmund Freud believed that childhood trauma influences and shapes who we become later in adulthood. He may have had a point. My obsession with men developed very early in my childhood. I was masturbating by the age of three and dreaming of detailed weddings with random boys in my classes by the age of five.

Does that mean I am crazy though?

Or does that mean the lack of romance and love between my parents drove me to find romance and love on my own, through any means possible?

Growing up around two people who constantly bickered and fought drove me away from them and straight into the arms of strangers. Having a father who was never available or attentive drove me to search for men who were. I fell for men who listened and were present despite whether I was attracted to them. I chased after assholes because they payed attention to me despite their incentives behind it. I convinced myself that anger and abuse from men mean passion and love. The more I was hated and emotionally abused, the more I felt loved.

What the fuck, right!?

Who does this?

Who says this?

Who equates getting punched in the eye with love?

Growing up, my family expressed care and concern through yelling and hitting. Those were their ways of showing my brother and I that they cared and loved us enough to put in the effort to punish us. They reasoned that, if they did not love us, then they would not waste the time and energy to punish us.

Crazy & Obsessed
Addicted to Relationships

As a little girl, I believed them. From the age of two until the age of eighteen, whenever I was beat with a broom or with a chair, I told myself it was out of love. Whenever I was screamed at ferociously, I told myself that I deserved it.

In short:

Anger = Love

Abuse = Passion

Raise of Voice = Care and Attention

Those are the connections I am used to.

Those are the mantras I live my life by.

Those are the rules that I cannot stop following, no matter how hard I try.

I let people run over my life because I see control and manipulation as love, and therefore, I use the same methods on others.

It is disgusting.

It takes a terrible toll on the human psyche, and it drives insanity to devour minds. Humans are not meant to be controlled and manipulated because we are animals at heart.

We want the chance to roam free, make mistakes, and fall on our own accord.

Crazy & Obsessed
Addicted to Relationships

We want our thoughts to feel like they can expand.

We want to feel limitless rather than feel locked in a cage.

When someone ignores or rejects us, they are in control.

We give them permission to grab hold of our lives and twist them into whatever they want.

We allow others to run the controller on how we can feel and how we should behave.

When they ignore us, we feel sad.

When they text us, we feel ecstatic.

When they leave us, we become devastated.

We need to stop giving others so much power where they become our puppeteer.

We are not puppets; we should not be controlled by someone we have just met.

We have known ourselves our entire lives, yet we let strangers waltz in and screw us over in a split second!

Some people actually commit suicide because of breakups.

From an outsider's perspective, we assume that these people have more internal psychotic issues going on than just a simple breakup.

That is a false perception.

Crazy & Obsessed
Addicted to Relationships

Breakups can be fatal.

They mess with every emotion and feeling that we have, translating into physical symptoms. As I mentioned before, when people experience heartbreak, their hearts can literally break. They can feel like they are dying, their arteries feel like they are clogging up, and they find it difficult to breathe. Their stomachs sink and their chests begin to compress, similar to symptoms of heart attacks.

When people say that they would rather die than continue to experience the pain of a breakup, they mean it.

They are not just being overdramatic.

The feelings that come with heartbreak can become so severe that even death seems like the better alternative.

Feeling suicidal after a breakup is not limited to a certain demographic. Anyone can experience it, despite the color of our skin, despite our financial status, despite the family we grew up in, despite our intelligence, and despite our relationship history.

We like to joke about people who have "crazy eyes" and how that is seen as a red flag. We steer clear of certain people based on appearances, and we judge others without giving them the chance to tell their stories or explain their situations.

Sometimes the ones we judge are the ones we need in our lives.

Sure, they have had rough pasts but so has everyone.

Crazy & Obsessed
Addicted to Relationships

Some people are just more open and honest about their pasts than others.

Some people hide their crazy until AFTER they have locked us in, only unleashing it when we have already invested.

Others show their crazy early on but end up being the ones who are caring and kindhearted.

Terrible situations can turn any person into a mental case.

Just because someone has had a rough past does not mean they deserve a rough future.

Just because someone has a history of suicide does not mean he/she is going to act on it.

Just because someone has had a terrible relationship and has made mistakes in the past, does not mean the same sequence of events will repeat again.

We do not know where people come from, therefore, we should not assume the worst. If we do, everyone would be single. Scars make people beautiful, and if we reject people based on those scars, we deserve to be alone.

The reason I want to share this little insight on suicidal behaviors after devastating situations is because I know, all too well, how difficult it is to not want to pull the trigger when all we feel, day and night, is immense pain. I was not a sane or clear-headed person during my intense periods of heartbreak, where all I wanted to do was die. I was not in a place where I could respectfully give myself to someone else.

Crazy & Obsessed
Addicted to Relationships

I was a mess, and my mind was cluttered; it all felt too unbearable to carry on. I do not go into relationships PLANNING to unleash my craziness, manipulate people, and make their lives miserable. I care about people. I am loving, patient, and I am an extreme people pleaser, but when I get hurt, I get angry, and that is when the switch happens.

Some may call it "bipolar," but I call it, "you-fucking-hurt-me-so-I-am-allowed-to-be-angry."

Pain is expressed in so many ways; it does not just involve crying and shutting others out. Those are what caused the pain to happen in the first place when all we wanted was to be heard.

Suicide is a cry for attention, a drastic measure to get people to listen to us and see that we need help.

Unfortunately, many of us still see suicide as a coward's way out, a selfish act of giving up and leaving loved ones behind to deal with the mess.

Chapter Twenty-Four

Are We Just Not Good Enough?

"We can only stand tall and proud if we allow ourselves to fall and crumble. Most days we will feel like shit, but all we need is one moment to prove our greatness." ℒ

No matter how hard and how much we try to distract ourselves from the feelings and emotions that rush over us when we remember all the pain and agony we have endured while in the state of "love" and constant obsession, we will ALWAYS be pulled back.

Accept it.

We will experience times where we seem fine, enjoying the things we love alone, regardless of what others think, but one second can lead to the next, and we find ourselves, once again, in constant turmoil and anxiety over people who make plans for dates and ghost us instead.

We text and we call.

We try to be respectful.

We try confrontation.

We try demanding answers.

We even try patience.

But patience can only last so long when "busy" equates to leaving us dry for three weeks and counting.

We live in an era where everyone is glued to their phones, whether they like to admit it or not. When we text people, regardless of how busy they are, they usually respond within twenty-four hours of receiving it, that is, if they wanted to respond.

I will admit it.

I have done this.

Crazy & Obsessed
Addicted to Relationships

I have read texts and blatantly ignored them just because I did not feel like talking.

However, being on the other side makes you realize how much it hurts.

When someone texts us, it is usually because they genuinely want to talk to us, see how we are doing, connect, and find out more about us, except for maybe the occasional "DTF?"

It takes effort and courage to pick up that phone, choose our names out of the contact list, and type out the message, which can sometimes be deep, personal, and embarrassing. When we ignore them, it leaves them with many lingering thoughts.

"Why are they not responding to me?"

"What could they possibly be so busy with that they cannot send back a simple reply?"

"Did I do something to piss them off?"

"Did I do something to hurt them?"

"What the fuck did I do?"

"Are they over me already?"

"Are they talking to someone else?"

"I bet they are fucking talking to a bunch of other fucktards right now."

Crazy & Obsessed
Addicted to Relationships

"What the fuck is wrong with me?!"

"Do they hate me that much that they cannot even give me the decency and respect of TELLING me that they are not interested?"

"WHAT THE FUCK DID I DO!?!"

It hurts fifty times WORSE to NOT say anything than to let people know that we are not interested. Yes, rejection hurts, but we believe that if the rejections are not direct, then we spare others of hurt feelings, and that by ghosting people, it slowly weans them off us and eventually both parties move on and neither side remembers any of it.

NO!

What REALLY HAPPENS when we ghost someone is that, although we may feel nothing, or we may feel free and capable of moving on, the person who was ghosted becomes stuck in constant anxiety. Regardless of how long two people have known each other and regardless of the status of the relationship, not knowing what is going on is one of the worse cycles of emotions anyone can go through. It is not cut and dry, where the person being rejected immediately gets the hint and moves on. It is a never-ending constant mind battle.

Regardless of how strong and independent we are, we still struggle with the demon of the "what ifs."

The person who rejected us did not just reject us.

They left us feeling unworthy, unloved, and undeserving of respect as if our lives did not matter.

Crazy & Obsessed
Addicted to Relationships

We begin to doubt our self-confidence.

We begin to wonder whether we are good enough to be respected at all.

We begin to wonder what we have done to deserve this type of treatment.

Why is it so common for people to do this?

Has there been evidence in their pasts that makes them believe that ghosting is the best plan of action?

Are they that cowardly that they cannot even send one text?

People are literally hiding behind their phones.

What is the worst that can happen?

They send a rejection text, and the person being rejected leaps through his/her phone and poltergeist out from the other side?

At least send the text and immediately proceed to blocking to avoid confrontation.

It is still a terrible thing to do, but at least the other person gets closure.

It will hurt, but at least it will hurt less.

Sometimes, even this is too much for people.

Crazy & Obsessed
Addicted to Relationships

So, where does that leave us? Some still ponder and obsess over "the one who got away" or "the one who could have been." Others fall back into own habits, settling for people they do not even like and crumbling into pieces when they eventually get rejected, letting the power of others destroy them.

How is it that someone, whom we have only known for a short period of time, can change our entire lives, alter our perspectives of love and ourselves, and leave us feeling empty and unfulfilled so quickly and so easily?

I once knew an actor, very responsive, great personality, and what seemed like a deep connection. The first date ended well. We made plans, went our separate ways, and ended the night with promising conversation.

Then it all fell apart.

No answer, no responses, no more of the daily conversations we used to exchange back and forth.

So, naturally, I thought:

"What the fuck is going on?"

"How can someone who seemed to like me ignore me so quickly?

"Did he die?"

"Did I say something wrong?"

"Was there something in my teeth?"

Crazy & Obsessed
Addicted to Relationships

I then proceeded to ask him:

"Hey, haven't heard back from you."

"Did I do something wrong?"

"Did I scare you away?"

"Do you not want to talk anymore?"

"Are you ghosting me?"

"If you do not like me, can you at least tell me?"

While this all seem like normal conversational behaviors for the victims of ghosting, they apparently appear as a crazy act of obsession for the ghoster.

No answer.

For SEVEN days.

Then, a response.

"Not ghosting you. I'm overwhelmed by the texting. You can still text me, but if I don't respond IMMEDIATELY, don't FREAK out."

"Okay, first, there is a HUGE GAP between texting back IMMEDIATELY and texting back ONE WEEK LATER. I know you have your phone on you because I have STALKED you enough to know your social media activity so do not even dare pin this on me."

That was what I should have said.

Crazy & Obsessed
Addicted to Relationships

But, being the timid person that I am, I responded with, "Of course! Take all the time you need! I'm patient! Please let me know if you need anything! Good luck at your acting conference!"

I said that over three weeks ago…

Now, I know I am not an actor, so I do not know the exact glitz and details of what the life of an actor looks like (mind you, not even a Hollywood actor, just some local dude trying to act like a big shot), but I need to know, IS THREE WEEKS THE DEFINITION OF "NOT IMMEDIATELY"???

I get that you do not want to be overwhelmed with text messages, but I have not sent one in four days!

Two sentences a day, three days a week, are too much!?

I know I call myself "crazy," but I really tried for this guy.

Normally, after one week, I would have blown up his phone with psychotic messages demanding answers until he proceeded to block me, but this time I waited.

Waited.

And waited.

And waited.

And waited….

Oh, but do not worry, the crazy did not go away just because I liked him; the crazy became stronger BECAUSE

Crazy & Obsessed
Addicted to Relationships

I liked him, so I tried replacing him any way I could. I tried to get him out of my head by talking to twenty other people, hoping one of them could replace him. I hooked up with as many people as I could, but that only left me feeling disgusted with myself.

It is often the ones who walk over our lives the least that leave the biggest marks.

We strive for answers because we are innately curious. We want what we cannot have, what we cannot know and, for some of us, we chase this fantasy that we must know every thought of every person we encounter.

We meet someone new, get married, have a family, grow old, and still, we are left with this feeling of wanting to know why our past lovers rejected us, what was wrong with us, whether the person we are with now is just someone we have settled for, and what our lives would have looked like if we had ended up with our exes instead?

Would that have made us happy?

Would anything have made us happy?

We will always have this itch in our hearts that make us doubt every decision we have ever made. The life we are living right now has been decided by a chain of events that led us up to this very moment.

Feelings are ever-changing.

Crazy & Obsessed
Addicted to Relationships

We think we can be happy if only we had this "person," if only we were "married," or if only we had what everyone else "has."

These are only transient materialistic "things" that can never truly justify happiness for us because we do not know what will make us happy. We see others "happy," and we assume it is because of the things they have, but people are also fantastic at hiding their true emotions and their problems.

When my ex broke up with me, the only thing I could focus on was getting him back, how happy I would be if he was in my life again, and how everything would be perfect if I can just see him again. But that was just my mind clouded with what I wanted AT THAT MOMENT.

And I got that moment.

I got him back.

I believed my life was perfect again… for a whole two weeks until it wasn't, and I became more miserable than I was before because I made promises I did not believe in to get back something I did not want.

I got what I wanted.

But I was still miserable.

We all try so hard to recover, so hard to take back our lives, until asshole number six comes along and ruins it for us all over again.

Crazy & Obsessed
Addicted to Relationships

We spend thousands of dollars on therapy and meditation classes to try and detox from the obsessions and negativities of toxic relationships.

We give ourselves positive affirmations daily to boost our self-esteem.

We date ourselves and attempt to meet only decent people rather than players.

We spend more time with friends and family to distract ourselves from overbearing loneliness.

We travel around the world to fall in love with our surroundings rather than rely on others.

We develop new hobbies, make career changes, and move to new cities to start over.

We delete social media and completely stop dating so we can piece ourselves back together.

But then he comes along.

With his perfect smile, gorgeous body, dazzling personality, and just like that, all our hard work goes straight into the trash.

We fall back into pretentious and non-existing love.

He breaks our hearts into a million pieces.

He throws us back into the dump we just picked ourselves out of.

Crazy & Obsessed
Addicted to Relationships

We pretend we are fine, brush ourselves off, and try to keep it together.

We tell ourselves that we WILL NOT engage in our obsessive behaviors.

We write reminders on our mirrors.

We carve them into our skins.

We deny that the craziness is still inside us.

We crack.

We rejoin social media.

We pull out our stalking resources.

We pop in a chick flick.

We go to town.

Scrolling through "Mr. Perfect's" Instagram page, wondering what the girl in his arm has that we do not.

Thinking:

"I just spent the past five years of my life improving all the qualities I can possibly improve and constructing myself into a "perfect" being, and I am STILL being rejected?!"

"What the hell?"

"What the hell did I do this time?"

Crazy & Obsessed
Addicted to Relationships

"What is wrong with me now!??"

"That is it."

"I give up."

"I will never get the guy."

"I will be a loser for the rest of my life because I suck."

"Nothing I do will ever be good enough."

"What the fuck does she have that I do not?!"

Truly, but unfortunately, this thought process rings all too well for most of us. It sucks to swallow the fact that, most of the time, two people are just not meant to be. The sparks are just not there, and the people we want may just have better connections with others than they do with us regardless of appearances or intelligence.

Not everyone we want is going to want us back, just like we do not want everyone who wants us.

There are going to be people who reject us just like there are going to be people we reject. But it does NOT mean that we are worthless. It does NOT mean that we are not perfect because perfection lies in our subjective perceptions of ourselves. It does NOT mean that our last five years were a waste of life because we learn and grow with each terrible dating experience.

We may not realize it in the moment, but with each rejection, we slowly learn how to recover with less pain. We cannot compare ourselves with the ones chosen over us because, in the end, it may have just not been the right fit, and it is better that we realize it sooner than later.

Somewhere on the other end, some people are wishing that they are us, just as we are wishing that we are not.

When the right people come along, we become perfect in their eyes no matter what we do. But we are to blame for the assholes we let in. We choose who we let in, and we choose who we keep out. For most of us, attractiveness and intelligence drive us toward certain people, i.e., the assholes and the bitches. We want people who look like models despite their moral characters because

We believe that being with gorgeous people will make us gorgeous by default and,

We believe that if we do not date people "up to standard" physically, then we would be judged for having low standard.

There has always been an unwritten criterion in terms of the types of partners we should have: men should be physically strong and fit to play the role of the breadwinner while women should be petite and pretty to play the role of the loyal housewife and caretaker.

We have taken this socially-constructed idea of the body type we SHOULD be looking for while casting aside everyone else.

We have replaced objective eyes with a checklist that we mark off as different people enter and leave our lives.

Crazy & Obsessed
Addicted to Relationships

We tell ourselves and others that we want someone with a kind and caring heart rather than a pretty shell, but time after time, we continue to chase based on our shallow desires.

Despite knowing the truth, we still falsely believe that we only want deep and sincere connections. When we are rejected or endure a broken heart, we play victim, in that we "never saw it coming," when we knowingly choose partners with higher risks of leaving.

We pretend we are the innocently-rejected because we do not want to admit that we fucked up again by choosing Prince Charming over the Pauper.

We want others to feel sorry for us and hate all the other prince charmings because it makes us feel better for our poor decisions.

We want others to NOT have Prince Charming because we hate the idea of our friends having "Mr. Hottie" while we settle for "Mr. Mediocre."

We secretly want everyone to be as miserable as we are, and we hate the idea of someone else having what we do not.

We should be happy for others because they are happy, not only when we are happy also.

Jealousy and hate exude more power than gratitude.

Chapter Twenty-Five

We Are All Closet Sociopaths

"We are all sociopaths. Some of us are more honest about it. Some of us deny it by exuding all opposite behaviors. We can only keep the truth hidden for so long before it all comes spilling out." ℒ

Take single women in their 40s, for example. They find joy in drinking wine and bitching about how all the men they have dated suck, and how women who marry in their

Crazy & Obsessed
Addicted to Relationships

20s will have rude awakenings when their men leave them in ten years for younger chicks.

*Note: I am only using "single women in their 40s" as an example. This can apply to all ages, genders, and relationship status.

The purpose of "bitch-speak" is to make people feel less ashamed of themselves. However, "bitch-speak" also forms a bond between people. Hating a specific type of people or a specific relationship status is what brings people together. It is very rare that human beings connect through positivity and sincere joy for each other; it is often a connection based on a common hatred for others. We struggle with being sincerely happy for other people because we are competitive by nature.

When we are happy, we want to be happier than everyone else.

When we are sad, we want others to be more miserable than us.

We even go as far as manipulating others into feeling terrible about themselves and lying about what their partners do in attempts to break them up.

We are not proud of it.

But it works.

Because the end goal is to make ourselves feel better, despite what it takes and, most of the time, we accomplish that, even if we consciously ruin the lives of others.

Crazy & Obsessed
Addicted to Relationships

Friendships form tighter when two newly single people come together rather than when two people in separate relationships come together.

When I was in the midst of one of my obsessive chases over men, I hated it when people I knew were happy in relationships. I Facebook stalked one of my exes, found out that he was in a serious relationship, and contacted him, not having spoken to him for over two years and fully knowing that he still had feelings for me. I played it off as "just wanting to catch up" but really, I wanted him to see me, realize how much he still loved me, cheat on his current girlfriend with me, and break up with her for me, just so I can REJECT HIM and FEED MY EGO by knowing I was still wanted.

I knew what I was doing was manipulative and pure evil, but I did it anyway because how I felt at that moment was much stronger than any moral compass buried inside my head.

At that moment, it felt like THE ONLY THING THAT WOULD MAKE ME FEEL BETTER WAS TO BREAK THEM UP.

At that moment, all I wanted to do was make someone else feel worse than I did despite what it took.

At that moment, I wanted to destroy all love, and because I had the power to do so, I went for it.

At that moment, I found joy in telling his girlfriend that he cheated on her while playing it off as an act of humanitarianism.

At that moment, I knew there was definitely something wrong with me, but I just DID NOT CARE.

At that moment, I felt guilty but proceeded anyway.

At that moment, I was flawed.

At that moment, I was broken.

We never want to admit our flaws because that would mean that we are flawed.

We find it difficult to accept that there is nothing wrong with being a little different, making mistakes, and occasionally falling.

Chapter Twenty-Six

Pick Yourself Up!

"Do you really want your ex to see you lying on the sidewalk, dirty, sad, and pathetic? Who cares if you feel like crap? Pick yourself off the disgusting ground, slap a smile on your face, and pretend that you own the world!" ℒ

We oversee how we deal with failure, how we deal with imperfections, and how we bounce back after tragedies.

Crazy & Obsessed
Addicted to Relationships

No one will ever go through life without falling.

We are all flawed, and we are all going to make mistakes whether big or small.

We can either choose to mope in our failures and let our lives be controlled by them, or we can choose to acknowledge that we are all messed up and do something about it.

We can choose to break the patterns that we are living, as hard as that may be.

We can choose to be the person that we strive to be rather than just pretending that we are.

We may not be able to stop obsessing over and craving attention from whoever we can find, but we can start by putting the phone down.

Download that app, flirt with as many people as you want, but put the phone down when the urge comes up to either go out on that date with that person you do not even like (because you know you will just end up fucking him/her and getting too attached), or to nonstop message someone you do like just because he/she has not responded in a few days.

The latter is very controversial. Depending on who we are, some of us get worried when people do not respond within a day, and for others, we are perfectly fine with not hearing from people for two weeks.

TWO WEEKS??!!

Crazy & Obsessed
Addicted to Relationships

Do you know what you can do in two weeks??!

You can quit your job!

In all seriousness, two weeks is the right amount of time to begin forgetting about people and move on, especially if we are on apps where we are chatting up multiple people at a time. If people do not respond to our messages within two weeks, they are either dead or clearly not interested. We know which of the two I am.

Ask yourself why you are talking to these people, why you are considering meeting up with them, whether you only swiped right because you are lonely or because you actually like them, whether you are only talking to them to forget about a recent breakup, and what intentions you have going into these dates.

We may be crazy and obsessive, but we are also resilient.

We may not know the right time to fight versus the right time to quit, but we do know how to bounce back after seemingly endless failures.

We FEEL like we will never recover.

We FEEL like we want our lives to be over when the person we are currently crushing on refuses to return our texts.

We FEEL like we will never love again after someone breaks out hearts.

We FEEL like we want to give up and are not strong enough to continue.

Crazy & Obsessed
Addicted to Relationships

But our feelings can be WRONG.

Our feelings can deceive and manipulate our thoughts and actions in ways we can never imagine.

And we let them.

Feelings are strongest when we are most vulnerable, so we engage in behaviors that would be insane to us otherwise. We are all intelligent people who know that our feelings do not define us, yet when we are broken, that logic no longer exists.

But what if these "feelings" did not exist?

What if, instead of becoming emotional over heartbreaks or other tragic incidents, we become fully logical?

What if we experience a painful breakup, and instead of breaking down in tears and anger, we simply acknowledge it and move on?

However, there are also complications and consequences for turning off our feelings. People actively choose to become indifferent, apathetic, and unemotional after breakups. There are classes, clubs, organizations, and self-help books and videos on how to remove emotional pain IMMEDIATELY post-breakup.

They challenge people to numb themselves, prepare for the worse at the very START of the relationship, expect everything to go wrong until proven otherwise, and if the relationship falters, they would have already been prepared, well-equipped to deal with and cease any pain that comes with heartbreak.

Crazy & Obsessed
Addicted to Relationships

But is this what we want?

Pain is painful, yes, it is in the word, but with pain, also comes a soul, a person, and a unique life. We think we want to forget and become numb to avoid feeling pain. We think forgetting and not caring will make us able to move on quicker and skip the five stages of breakups that almost all people go through.

But what do the five stages of grieving after a breakup mean? Denial, anger, bargaining, depression, and acceptance are all critical stages in learning and building ourselves whole again after being torn down. Most people look at these stages, dread the first four, and quickly want to move onto acceptance.

But moving onto acceptance right away takes away our chances to learn from our mistakes, to learn the types of people that we can and cannot get along with to avoid making the same mistakes, and to learn more about what we want in a person as opposed to our physical impulses and external attractions.

So, what are the consequences of turning off our feelings rather than just letting them flow through us?

When we turn off our emotions and how we feel toward situations, we experience a lack of emotional and physical pain that can prove as life-saving. Normally, when we experience mental pain such as heartbreak, our minds and bodies take in this information and learn from it:

The types of triggers that cause us to react emotionally,

Crazy & Obsessed
Addicted to Relationships

How quickly or slowly our bodies react to different situations and,

How our bodies recover and the time it takes to do so.

We subconsciously store information based on each interaction or relationship with people, so when we enter back into the dating world, we actively screen out those who remind us of our pasts. We avoid people who have similarities to those who have hurt us, and we gravitate toward people who have similarities to those who have loved us.

When we remove the pain, we are no longer able to recognize and screen out the people who will hurt us. We put ourselves in a place of high risk and danger because we can no longer recognize signs that our pasts have given us.

When we train ourselves to become emotionless and stop feeling, we lose the quality that makes us human: empathy. When we stop feeling, we also stop caring, and we end up turning off our emotions toward everyone around us, good and bad, and we become soulless. Turning off our emotions means we are telling ourselves and others that we do not care and do not want to care.

Chapter Twenty-Seven

The Face Behind The Mask

"Behind every smile is a tear. Behind every dollar is debt. Behind every story is a lie. Behind every person is another person crying for help." ℒ

It is common to see suicidal ideations and behaviors as signs of weakness because we tend to see them as signs of giving up and selfishly leaving behind loved ones to deal with OUR MESS. Even though we will never know the true story behind those who go through with suicide, those who have been at their breaking points and have come down from the ledge know what it means to truly become the heroes of their own lives.

Wanting to die is a result of absolute pain and an influx of overwhelming feelings that are no longer able to be controlled. Wanting to die is the last resort from dealing with pain because the means to cope are no longer present.

Suicide can be a result of many reasons, but one of the main reasons why suicide happens too often is because those around us have either chosen to cease their brains from experiencing painful emotions or are actively hiding their own pain and thus, lose that empathetic connection with us where they are no longer able to understand why people can feel suicidal, turn to judgment instead of empathy, and make us feel even more isolated and unsupported.

When we are at the brink of suicide and decide to choose life instead, that is a sign of turning off these powerful emotions.

When we recover from a painful breakup without having to get under someone else, that is a sign of turning off these powerful emotions.

When we stop our tears midway through crying, brush ourselves off, and walk out the door to deal with life, we are turning off these powerful emotions.

Crazy & Obsessed
Addicted to Relationships

When we are finally able to wake up, still feel incredibly overwhelmed with pain and NOT climb back into bed, we are turning off these powerful emotions.

For those who have experienced many, or even one, powerful breakup(s), how do we know if the next person we meet is right for us? There can be pieces of them that resonate with our long list of desires, or they can even check off our entire list, but how do we TRULY KNOW? Just because someone seems right, feels right, and is, hypothetically, everything we have always wanted, does not guarantee that he/she is not like those who have hurt us in our pasts.

How do we know when we are no longer confusing love with infatuation? How do we know when we have found the ones we want to be with and are not just blinded by desperation? This is the problem with having a brain that never stops adapting and changing.

We never truly know what we want.

We know what we want based on the knowledge of what we DO NOT WANT. When we experience a situation or a person that has hurt us, we know we do not want to go back to that.

But is this enough?

Is screening out the negatives enough to see the positives?

The process of elimination only works if we have exhausted every possible option of pain that has ever existed or will exist. We cannot choose who our next partner(s) will be based on who we think we do not want.

Crazy & Obsessed
Addicted to Relationships

For example, everyone behaves differently during the first date, exaggerating the positives and shadowing the negatives. We want to show off our best qualities and hide the worst. We make up white lies to enhance our portfolios, and we shove everything else inside a box and chuck it into the river, making us seem like the "perfect specimen" rather than the "average Joe." We do this again, and again, and again, and again, only showing our true selves AFTER years of dating.

By then, our brains have become so adapted to the lies that others have shown that we become blinded when their flaws begin to appear. We can be burning in fire but still only see the flowers we have been given on day one. We can never know if the next person we meet is right for us because we do not know when someone is lying and when they are not, especially when they are good at it. We do not know if the "good" impressions that they make are really who they are.

We cannot trust the words of anyone unless their actions continue to prove them true. Everyone can be a liar. Some people still lie forty years into a marriage, and it is something that can or cannot be controlled by the liars themselves.

When we love someone or want to impress someone, we cannot help but subconsciously exaggerate who we are based on who we want to be or who we think the other person wants us to be.

Chapter Twenty-Eight

Blind Love

"If we never open our eyes, we never see the ugly truth of what we cannot have. Our perceptions only exist if our minds become weak enough to allow it." ℒ

I recently met someone who I thought I really wanted to be with. We seemed perfect together. Everything felt right, similar interests and personalities, and I wanted to say and do everything I could to impress him. When he ended date number one on a high note and ignored me indefinitely, I continued to pine over and chase after him.

When he scheduled date number two, five months later, I still thought we had a chance. When he texted back after nine weeks of hiatus, I believed I loved him. When he kept postponing our third date for an additional eight months, using work as an excuse and running off to a concert in Canada with another girl when he deemed "too busy," I FINALLY realized what I was doing.

I was chasing after "blind love."

Blind love is when we become so infatuated with strangers that we feel like we are "in love" even though we have just met them and know nothing about them. Blind love is when we intensely want to be with and love someone despite any red flags or negative consequences. Blind love is when we fantasize about spending the rest of our lives with someone after only the first date.

However, blind love is not necessarily a bad thing. Blind love can be dangerous, but blind love can also mean passion. When we fall in love with our instincts rather than our logic, we prevent ourselves from checking qualities and people off a checklist. We follow what we FEEL we want rather than what we SHOULD want.

We block out external judgments and reasoning that may prevent us from loving freely. Unfortunately, blind love is only passionate if we DO NOT cross the border over into obsessive love. We can blindly fall in love with someone at first sight, but DO NOT let the other person know because then it can become fatal.

Crazy & Obsessed
Addicted to Relationships

We can fall in love with someone, but then STEP BACK and monitor the signs to ensure that is what we want. We can wear our hearts on our sleeves, but BE SMART enough to not give ourselves to just anyone. We can fall in love at first sight, but when they reject us, know that we were at least passionate enough to take that RISK in the first place.

Chapter Twenty-Nine

What Is Jealousy?

"Jealousy is wanting what we already have, loving what we already hate, living what we already dream." ℒ

For most, jealousy is "insecurities manifesting into selfish acts that tear apart happy relationships." Jealousy is not selective to certain groups of people; jealousy hits everyone, and when it does, it hits us hard. Even the most confident and secure deal with the anxiety that is jealousy when it comes to someone they love.

Jealousy can creep in at all angles; men tend to be more jealous of physical connections with a third party while women tend to be more jealous of emotional connections with a third party.

Although jealousy has been shown to be a healthy emotional dynamic for people in serious relationships, jealousy is not commonly seen as a healthy expression. For example, when two people are "in love," and by that, I mean with completely healthy and balanced levels of communication and understanding, jealousy is a healthy emotion, where one person expresses his/her feelings and reasoning while the other person acknowledges, accepts it, and both parties work together to compromise and figure out a way to reduce that level of jealousy.

However, as we all know, relationships generally do not work that way. In most relationships, when one person expresses how he/she feels, the other person feels attacked and gets extremely defensive, making the level of jealousy even worse because now it seems like the partner has something to hide.

The expression of jealousy itself is not a sign of mistrust. When jealousy is not accepted well by the other party, it turns into mistrust on both sides. The person to whom the jealousy is being expressed, feels accused despite having a reason to or not, and becomes defensive. The person who is expressing the jealousy feels as if the other person has something to hide by becoming defensive rather than being open and becomes paranoid and neurotic that his/her feelings are being ignored and avoided.

When this occurs, trust cannot be resolved. Both parties can try, but there will always be this lingering feeling of whether the other person is still faithful or not, and hence, will eventually cause more and more accusations.

When jealousy is not properly accepted, it can also act as a trigger for impending acts of infidelity. When people are being accused of doing something that they are not doing, their minds instinctively go to the rebellion and the "I'll show you" mode. They begin to have the mindset that, if someone is already accusing them of doing something, and therefore, somewhat believes that it is already happening, they might as well just do the act they are being accused of because there is essentially nothing left to lose.

When jealousy is not well accepted, people become consumed with jealousy until they eventually tear relationships apart with neediness and mistrust or with anger and pain. Relationships can never work when jealousy meets aloof. Jealousy is inevitable in relationships, but relationships can be saved from it with understanding, and that is what everyone in any kind of relationship should strive for, whether romantic, familial, or social, because all "negative" emotions can be resolved when both parties understand the situations and are willing to work though the negativity.

Jealousy is also commonly known to occur ONLY when more than one party is involved. What if I told you that jealousy can happen within oneself, that we can essentially be jealous of ourselves? We can be jealous of

Crazy & Obsessed
Addicted to Relationships

the person we really are, the person we fear we are not allowed to be.

Our whole lives, we have been fed messages, either from our parents, the media, or our local communities, that we pretty much suck as ourselves and can only ever make it if we become someone else. And so, we listen, and we become someone else, only to the detriment of ourselves and the benefit of no one.

Not one single person benefits from us changing our demeanor and derailing from our true persons, but everybody loses as a result.

WE LOSE because we deprive ourselves from the chance of discovering the beautiful soul we were born to be, throwing out our uniqueness and becoming spawns of robots instead, and EVERYONE ELSE LOSES because they miss out on the chance to experience the amazing person we can be if given the freedom to do so.

Every person has a special heart that distinguishes them from the normality of the social world, and because of this, we develop the capacity to love ourselves and others. When we deprive ourselves from being the person we were born to be, we lose this ability and can no longer truly love outside of deception, so we lie because living in lies is all we know.

However, the longer we pretend to be someone we are not, the more we begin to realize that being someone else is FUCKING BORING! Who wants to go through their entire lives, following in the footsteps of someone else, and never having the chance to blossom outward or have their own say in any aspect of their own lives?

Crazy & Obsessed
Addicted to Relationships

We all secretly want to be different and unique, but unfortunately, society still shuns on those who do deviate from the norm because WE LET IT. We become jealous of ourselves when we feel that itch inside of us wanting to break free, struggling to push its way out. We want our individualities to shine but fear they will be rejected.

We become jealous of the "us" we dream about at night, the only way we can visualize who we want to be without social criticisms. But jealousy of the self is a motivator! We want to be jealous of ourselves because it means we love ourselves enough to feel envy. We want that jealous feeling to shine stronger so it gives us the extra push we need to overcome our fears and bring out the inner soul that we have been hiding our whole lives.

Jealousy is a strong emotion that drives desires and actions into fruition. When we are jealous of someone else, almost nothing can keep us from acting on this emotion until we quell it. When we become jealous of ourselves, our human instincts, despite social influences, will stop at nothing to quell this jealousy.

Chapter Thirty

We Are Selfish Assholes

"Humans love to play victim. We thrive on being the innocent who gets crushed by those we blame. We thrive on pretending to be the weak being destroyed by the strong. We are not victims. We are manipulative. We know exactly what to say at the exact moments to get what we want." ℒ

Have you ever felt so connected to someone that it feels almost like a dream when you are with that person?

Crazy & Obsessed
Addicted to Relationships

Have you ever felt so in love with someone that seeing that person makes you breathless, and the thought of that person leaving makes it difficult to breathe?

Have you ever met someone who swept you off your feet in mere seconds and made you feel like royalty?

Have you ever spoken to someone who brightens up your day, puts endless smiles on your face, and makes you feel protected from all the problems in your world?

We have all experienced this feeling of breathtaking love, where we fall for someone so hard that we cannot fathom our lives without them. Although some people have remained with their "soulmates" from their teens to old age, the rest of us have not been so lucky. The rest of us deal with this cycle of back and forth, from hopeful and in love to devastation and rejection, only to transfer that over to the next person, and the next, and the next.

This is not because we are incapable of holding onto a person or a relationship; this is because these fantasies and hallucinations we have that "love conquers all" or "meant to be" are all fake. This is not what love did to us; this is what standards and expectations did to us.

Our minds have become so convoluted by what love should look like and how love should feel like that we trick ourselves into "falling in love at first sight" just so we can experience this "moment" that everyone else around us seems to be experiencing. We have become so good at lying to ourselves that we do not see it until months, or even years, later that the person we are with is not the person we thought we fell in love with. True, it could be due to one person changing over time, but the

Crazy & Obsessed
Addicted to Relationships

main reason is that we do not know who we get into relationships with, and we do not know who we fall in love with.

This is because we have become blinded with our subjective perspectives when we enter new relationships. The man we think is the man of our dreams could very well be a mediocre person that we have plucked out and subconsciously molded into the vessel of our desires.

The more time we spend with just one person, the more we begin to visualize that person as the ONLY PERSON we want for eternity. We begin to see this single soul as the "savior" of our romantic lives. We begin to mentally mold this person, this person whom we may not have even found attractive among a crowd of others but suddenly do because everyone else is out of mind, into the person we have been looking for all along, and the only one we would ever be with.

Our illusion of how we think we see the person we are with, not only ruins our opportunity for real potential love, but it manipulates and uses the other person, robbing their chance of being with someone who ACTUALLY WANTS to be with them.

How can we stop something that we do not even realize we are controlling in the first place?

Is it even possible to stop ourselves from falsely loving someone when we are so prone to leading with our hearts instead of our brains?

How do we know that we are in the depths of it BEFORE it is too late?

Crazy & Obsessed
Addicted to Relationships

Can we learn to control our impulsive behaviors before they begin to control us?

We are not manipulative and terrible people.

We are people who have been told to behave in certain ways so many times that it has become instinctive. We have become so used to falling in "love" before falling in "like" that we have trained ourselves to rush into relationships before thinking. We not only begin to manipulate and brainwash others, but we also begin to brainwash ourselves.

The core of this problem is the need for validation.

When someone has feelings for us, but we do not necessarily feel the same way, we become addicted to the attention and the validation that this person gives us. We become obsessed with someone worshipping us that we do not even care who the person we are with is. We live in an age where we no longer fall in love with people themselves; we fall in love with what people are willing to give us and whether we believe that is enough.

When we fall in love with materialism and love selfishly, we set ourselves and others up for "infidelity without remorse." We lose our empathy for how someone feels, and we act based on what we want and ONLY WHAT WE WANT. We open doors to seek out other partners when the ones we have fail to give us everything we want.

When two people love each other, what they can and cannot offer each other is irrelevant. They love each other as the persons that they are despite the goods and services that they can provide. Love is not torn apart when one person refuses to become the "slave" of the other. It is only out of selfish love do we seek out other potential "slaves" that can continue the work of previous "slaves."

When people are in relationships where they report feeling unhappy and used, it is because they are.

We have become so independently focused that we seek out all aspects of life that can benefit, but not hurt, us. We run away from all, and any, sources of pain, ghosting and leaving behind others to deal with our betrayals and seek out other sources of pleasure. Because of this constant need for validation from others, the only way we can stop our patterns of manipulation and falling for people we do not actually want, is to simply TAKE A BREAK.

When we take a break from dating and relationships, we take a break from feeling the intense need to quickly get into one and do everything we can to control them into benefiting ourselves.

We can still form relationships with people, just not romantic ones that trigger our needs. We are half as likely to manipulate friends than we are to manipulate partners. Friends can come and go while partners are more intimate, so they are less likely to do all they can to please someone they like and trigger a dangerous path.

We need to stop feeding off the energy of others and start focusing on the energy we already have. When we spend so much time trying to control others and situations, we are expending more energy than our "victims," carefully crafting every word and every action, making sure we do not get caught. It is physically and mentally draining to control another human being, but we continue doing so because of the power that comes with it.

Why do we do this?

Insecurity.

Since the day we were born, we were told by everyone around us that we will never be good enough, that we will never amount to anything, and that we will always be alone if we decide to tackle life as the person we are right now. We have been told that we need to completely change our personas and become the opposite of who we are in order to be accepted by those around us. We are constantly being fed messages that the person we want to be is the person we should never be.

Girls are raised being told that they will never find husbands if they are independent and outspoken. Boys are raised being told that they must never be vulnerable and sensitive, or they will be socially rejected by their peers.

It used to be that, in order to remain in any sort of relationship, girls needed to be present but not heard, to be available despite what they were going through, to be serving and obedient despite how they were treated, and to always cater to and agree with their husbands to keep marriages alive. In modern days, this role has switched to men when it comes to keeping marriages alive, known as "happy wife, happy life."

Either way, every decade employs certain standards when it comes to keeping a relationship or a marriage intact, and people are expected to blindly follow them or face lonely lives. This puts people in positions where they are forced to completely surrender for the sake of others, for the sake of "togetherness," and for the sake of "everlasting happiness," or remain "unhappy."

How happy can we really be as slaves to someone else?

How can our happiness stem solely from the happiness of someone else?

How can we possibly justify to ourselves that the way we feel and the way we behave can ever be thrown into the control of a stranger?

Can we untrain our brains?

Can we unlearn the habits that have been subconsciously worshipped for generations?

Can we teach ourselves to steer away from succumbing to the confines of those around us and finally learn to take back our own lives?

Humans are capable of so many feats when it comes to striving as independents. We know how to grasp onto the things we want when it does not involve others. We are resilient, and we face all sorts of adversities, from withstanding negative degree weather to scaling insanely high peaks to crossing ferociously dry heats of deserts.

We fight physical scars caused by wars and mental scars caused by PTSD. We fight death every time we face uncertainties and step outside our comfort zones. We have been through violence and discrimination, but time after time again, we recover and bounce back.

Crazy & Obsessed
Addicted to Relationships

Then why is it so fucking difficult to tell the next asshole trying to control our lives to just back off?

Why do we live in a nation where people are so afraid of being alone that they will literally give up everything just to avoid feeling that way?

How is it that we can fight death but fear loneliness?

It is because we have been taught that defying death is awesome while remaining single is sad and pathetic. We are inherently social creatures who need to be around others so we feel needed and experience belonging. Dodging death is not in our inherent natures and, therefore, is seen as a great feat when avoided. When we fail to meet what is in our blood and expected of us, we become great failures to ourselves.

We have been told to grow up, marry well, and start a family; everything else we encounter along the way are just extras. But we can learn to detach ourselves from our emotions and avoid becoming slaves to strangers. By taking back our lives and avoiding serial dating, we train our brains to focus internally rather than externally.

We train ourselves to become more selfish toward ourselves and less vulnerable toward the selfishness of others. We can become selfish toward the self but remain compassionate toward others.

Loving someone does not mean completely surrendering.

Loving someone means finding equal balance between giving and taking without one side completely overpowering the other.

Crazy & Obsessed
Addicted to Relationships

Loving someone means looking out for ourselves before looking out for others because we can only give to others when we have finished giving to ourselves.

Depriving ourselves of the goodness that we can give ourselves is the ultimate cause of pain to our physical and emotional health. We lose sight of who we can be for ourselves, the lovers we can be for ourselves, when we are immersed in trying to keep someone around by making him/her happy just because we fear being alone.

We fear ending up as the old woman with the twenty cats or the old man who resents everyone so we would rather settle for a stranger, an unfamiliar, than face the possibility of feeling lonely.

But the fear is all in our heads!

We only fear ending up alone when we have not lived it personally. Those who have braved through the anxiety of this fear end up completely loving their solo lives, never regretting not having settled. We turn to infidelity in our 50s because we regret having settled in our 20s. We run away and start over because we cannot admit to ourselves that we have failed ourselves by placing our entire lives in the palm of someone else.

For years, we have lied to ourselves that the stable and comfortable lives that we have been living are the lives that we want. We endure abuse and misery for decades until we finally snap, and we either rebel against all that we have fought for, or we die with extreme regret on our death beds.

Crazy & Obsessed
Addicted to Relationships

If we learn to step out of our comfort zones and learn to live in the fear of uncertainty, even for just a little while, we prevent ourselves from both regretting and destroying our lives. If we cannot honestly say we are dedicated and happy with the person we are currently with, set him/her free so both are given the chance to find the person who we and them CAN be dedicated and happy with. Holding onto someone purely based on fear destroys the lives of many people: ourselves, our partners, and potential children involved.

We should not live in the mindset where we believe that it is okay to bring children into this world based on fear of being alone or based on societal pressure to belong and accommodate the standards others think we should live by. This only foresees neglect, lack of true love, regret, and worst of all, self-hate.

Short-term gratification can never exceed long-term sustained happiness, yet we let it take over, because at that time, it feels right. It becomes difficult for us to see beyond immediate pleasures, especially when we predict future pain.

We want to experience all the good before the bad gets a chance to reach us. So, we throw ourselves into destructive behaviors because, for a short while, they feel amazing with no IMMEDIATE CONSEQUENCES.

But what if we can foresee how our lives will turn out based on the decisions that we make?

How will we change our choices?

Will we even change how we decide on certain actions?

Crazy & Obsessed
Addicted to Relationships

Is knowing the future and the consequences certain actions will bring enough to steer us away from choosing based on immediate pleasures?

Or will we still fall into the trap of instant gratification?

Take another hypothetical scenario, further into the future. What if we can experience, first-hand, both the BENEFITS and the CONSEQUENCES of actions, and then turn back in time to make our decisions, fully knowing how each one feels like and the pros and cons each one brings. Will we alter our decision-making to avoid long-term consequences, or will we STILL make decisions that lead to instant pleasure?

Despite how much we know and how much experience we have, we will always make choices that lead to instant pleasure, instant happiness, and instant gratification, whether real or false, whether for ourselves or someone else. This is because of the constant fears of "what ifs."

WHAT IF the long-term happiness never comes?

WHAT IF I die before I get to experience the benefits of my choices?

WHAT IF I do not take the instant happiness and completely regret it later?

WHAT IF I do not settle and end up in misery for the rest of my life?

WHAT IF the person I rejected is the person I am meant to be with?

Crazy & Obsessed
Addicted to Relationships

WHAT IF this person was my true love, and now I will end up alone for the REST OF MY LIFE!?!?!?

WHAT IF!?

These "what ifs" are only results of insecurities. We only question our futures and the unknown because we doubt that life always has a way of working itself out. We always want to be in control of our own situations. We make immediate choices and impulsive decisions because we would rather our lives fail in our own hands than in the hands of others. We rush to self-sabotage before life can destroy our lives for us. We rush to settle for the unfamiliar before others can call us "fuck ups."

We deceive ourselves into falling in love just so we can avoid feeling alone. We have so much, yet so little, control over our own lives to the point where we blame ourselves when others take advantage of us and abuse us. When we give our power over to those we have become vulnerable enough to trust, we blame ourselves for doing so when we are betrayed.

However, we do not fail when we decide to become vulnerable. When we give ourselves and our hearts to other people, we are building ourselves up to become stronger and more successful people despite whether we are accepted or rejected.

When we open our delicate hearts to love, we are demonstrating enough courage to be able to put our hearts into the hands of others rather than remain in our comfort zones and hold our love in because we fear getting hurt. Even if we are rejected, we can at least stop blaming ourselves for "failure" and start congratulating ourselves for being courageous enough to share our lives despite the risks of getting hurt and damaged.

Unfortunately, when we open our true selves up to the world around us, we also become flooded with waves of insecurity. We immediately start questioning whether we made the right decision by sharing ourselves. We immediately start regretting having said anything at all because we can never be 100% positive what others will think or how they will respond.

It takes a lot to speak up first, fully knowing that we have a 50% chance of being turned down but doing it anyway. But why are we much more willing to be vulnerable when it comes to falling in love than when it comes to admitting that we messed up?

Why is it so much easier for us to risk insecurity when it comes to admitting happiness, love, and joy, but so hard when it comes to admitting shame and regret?

We are always surrounded by insecurities, in our jobs, our relationships, our family, and even within ourselves. We have the tendency to always put ourselves down just when things are looking up. We tell ourselves that we will never be good enough so when things do go wrong, we will have already prepared ourselves for the worst, and when things go right, we feel that much more elated.

Reverse psychology is a complete hoax.

Similar to pills and self-help books, we use it as a placebo to make ourselves believe the self-detrimental lies that we tell ourselves, self-prophesizing our negative thoughts. We only experience our insecurities if we believe in them;

otherwise, they just remain in hibernation inside our deepest subconscious and never flourish.

We bullshit ourselves with endless excuses of why it is okay to bash ourselves and our egos into the ground, and as a result, we willingly allow others to also bash us into the ground.

How can we stop our insecurities from ruining us when our entire lives have been filled with loved ones telling us that we should feel ashamed of ourselves, that we should doubt ourselves, and that the only way we can ever be accepted is to submit and obey?

Can we ever live a satisfied and fulfilled life without the constant worry of disappointing others and not living up to the social standards that society has created for us?

Chapter Thirty-One

All Work, No Play

"We share with others trauma that we would never wish on our worst enemies. What we fail to share is the strength that arises as a result of trauma. We have perished in the flames but have risen from the smoke. Surviving our deepest fears helps us fulfill our greatest dreams." ℒ

Crazy & Obsessed
Addicted to Relationships

Most of us can live out our entire lives without significant physical or psychological trauma: we learn, we work, we love, we grow old, and we die. It makes life easy, but going through life with these simple and mundane routines makes us never feel the drive to CHANGE. We never experience what it feels like to hit rock-bottom, but we also never experience what love can be like for us outside of having to rely on person X or person Y to give us fulfilling experiences.

Not having hit rock-bottom (in terms of love), not having been ghosted, not having been abused, not having been left at the altar, not having been cheated on, not having been mentally disrespected and destroyed, and not having been beaten to the point of no return, leave us feeling empty, unfulfilled, and ignorant to the many possibilities of love that can exist because content prevents us from exploring.

Not having been through relationship trauma keeps us in a place of mundane satisfaction, where we are not quite sure where we belong, where we have sporadic doubts of staying or leaving the people we are with, and where we feel an itch to find something else but never pull the trigger to do so.

When we are not completely satisfied with the moments that we are experiencing but have not been destroyed by them either, we remain stagnant in our unsatisfactory love lives, sleeping next to people we may have settled for and having happy moments with our partners only when we engage in activities such as lavish vacations, other people, alcohol, and parties. We become distracted from who we are with and never fully realize whether we actually love (or still love) those we are with or if we only tolerate them enough where we do not hate them.

Couples who fight, argue, and cheat constantly interact with each other, allowing each other to face the anger and animosity that one person feels toward the other, and eventually forcing them to realize whether they love each other enough to work through their problems or whether it is time to call it quits and search for other potential mates.

Couples who become bored of their partners but never feel the drive to speak up or take drastic action toward someone or something else, remain in silence and continue to feel the breaths of "what ifs" until the day they die.

We can love people but not be IN LOVE with them. We believe that if we love, i.e., care, we should avoid hurting those we love in any way, including leaving when we feel unfulfilled. We find it extremely difficult to turn people down because we associate "not the right fit" with "rejection" and "we are not good enough." We find it easier to ghost those we care about because we believe that it hurts less than rejection.

When people tell us that they do not want to be with us, we take it personally and blame ourselves for it even though that may not be true. Even the strongest of us can be destroyed by feelings of not being wanted. It will never feel good to be rejected because we see it with a negative connotation. We associate rejection with being "ugly," "hated," "stupid," and "unlovable" rather than seeing the situation as being given the chance to avoid something that would have turn out terribly if we continued to let the interaction/relationship continue.

It is only after we have found others better suited for us that we begin to acknowledge that the people we have been so obsessed with are simply passersby, a taste but not a meal, a touch but not a hold. Only when we are truly happy, do we see how foolish we were, obsessing over those who were never meant to be with us in the first place.

I used to be obsessed with someone who specifically clarified that he could NEVER be with me, and that all he was looking for were people to mess around with (he even called himself "a piece of man-meat"). However, I did not want to believe him. I tried to make him change his mind. I became obsessed with telling myself how he was perfect for me, and I spent every night dreaming about how great we would be together. I tried giving him everything he wanted, giving up my own values, losing my self-respect, and hating people I did not even know just because they were associated with him.

This broke me, but I pushed on. I continued to tell myself that if I just kept being patient, just kept being supportive, and just kept staying positive, that he will come around, that he will eventually change his mind, and that he will want to be with me. Three months, six months, a year went by, and it only resulted in him pulling further and further away from me, eventually posting a picture on Instagram of him together with another girl in California.

This truth smacked me in the face like I had expected but failed to accept, forcing me to look within and realizing what the fuck I was doing. I forced myself to finally give up on this person that I was in love and obsessed with.

There is a certain point in an obsession where you feel so destroyed and so hurt that there is no coming back from it. There is only so much hope you can have for someone when, time after time, they continue to treat you like garbage.

I have had more than my fair share of experiences when it comes to the horrible actions of other people, letting one person after the next shit all over me while I just took it with a smile, metaphorically. But I was naïve. I wanted to be loved and cared for so much that I pushed my self-esteem and self-respect aside so others can take what they wanted and all that they wanted, leaving me in the dust when they were finished while I ignorantly told myself that they still wanted me.

I started dating when I was about 19. It took me over 9 years of abuse and neglect to realize that I deserve to be treated like a human being, something obvious and sad for those on the outside looking in but a serious reality hit for those also going through the same experiences.

It is still a struggle; I do not have it all together, and many days, especially on the low lows, I still let myself fall into the trap of being used and abused, remembering to pull out just before it becomes too late. When you have become so accustomed to giving into others and living your life for the sole purpose of making the person in front of you or next to you happy, you fall into this pattern where you no longer know what to do with yourself or how to live with yourself when you are no longer obligated to abide by those "rules."

Crazy & Obsessed
Addicted to Relationships

To this day, even after pulling myself away from the toxic environments that I had created for myself and finding a relationship where I no longer chase, I still find myself full of insecurities. After having been with so many people who did not care about me and now finding someone who does, I continue to create a path of self-sabotage where I keep feeling like I do not deserve any of it. This never-ending feeling of insecurity ruins potentially amazing relationships, something I need to learn to break out of before ruining another.

However, before we can tackle and find healthy relationships, we need to work on ourselves and what it is we really want.

Is it a relationship we want, or do we just want to not be alone? Never get into any kind of relationship if it is the latter because it will only destroy you and the person you are with.

Hint: If you have recently come out of a relationship, whether healthy or toxic, you are not in a place where you are ready to tackle another one. You are in a place of limbo, where you have to figure out what it is that made the previous relationship end, how significant of a role you played in that, whether you will bring that same behavior or action to your next partner, whether you have flaws that you need to work on, and most importantly, whether you are actually ready to be with someone else or if you are only using new people as distractions from the old like the classic saying, "The best way to get over someone is to get under someone else."

So, when do we know if we are TRULY ready to move on, with a fresh perspective and a fresh start into a new relationship without constantly reminiscing the past? When we first get out of relationships, especially long-term relationships where we have so much history with our ex-partners, it is extremely difficult to separate anger from love.

When people leave us and break our hearts, or when we force ourselves to leave those we cared about, our minds become over-confluent with anger and confusion. All we can focus on is how much we hate our exes and how much we just want to get as far away from them as possible and move on.

So, we try, and we do, with finding a rebound as the most common way, latching onto said rebound, and deceiving ourselves into believing that we are actually in love with said rebound, when, more likely than not, we are only confusing love with the strong desire to forget. Some of us tell ourselves that we can completely separate anger from love. Some of us can even convince our rebounds that we are not confused.

When people leave serious long-term relationships, where they had so much love and care for their exes, and immediately try to jump back into the dating market without even waiting a week, they are looking for a distraction.

When people swear on their lives that they are completely over their exes and rush to start something new with strangers, they are looking for a way out.

When people say "I love you" within a month of dating, they are looking for a replacement.

Crazy & Obsessed
Addicted to Relationships

How long can we live in denial before we realize that we forgot to slow down and work on our pain before jumping into new potential pain? How long before it takes us to realize that we no longer "love" the people we are with because we never loved them in the first place? How long before we stop distracting who we are and what we want from ourselves with what we want from others? How long before we can reach the stage where we no longer rely on others to make us happy?

Because they cannot.

No one can truly make us happy if we are dissatisfied with ourselves.

Only we possess the power to quell the pain that persists within us.

Pain does not go away; pain can only be dealt with head on.

Crush the heartache that courses through our veins by acknowledging it.

Forgive those who hurt us so we do not take the pain out on others.

Remember that, at the end of the day, the only person we have left is ourselves.

We can never rely on the presence of another person to fulfill a need if we cannot fulfill that need ourselves. We need to stop bouncing from person to person, constantly seeking new people to fill the holes that are missing within. One person can never satisfy all that we need for ourselves; only we can fill in the missing gaps.

Hence, why so many of us become unfaithful. We keep trying to find that ONE PERSON who can give us EVERYTHING we need, and when we do not, when we find out that the person we thought we have found can only satisfy a fraction of the needs we desire, we seek out others to fill in the rest of the gaps, therefore, leading to infidelity. We know all too well what it feels like to cheat on our partners or have our partners cheat on us.

It sucks.

I get it.

We feel an immense sense of betrayal and anger running down our spines as we experience the wrath that results from the disloyalty of those we loved and trusted. We put our hearts into the hands of those who were once strangers, letting go of our own control and allowing others to take part in the lives we have constructed for ourselves.

When we say "I love you" for the first time to someone we still see as risky and untrustworthy, we are telling the other person that we see him/her as worthy enough to become vulnerable for.

When we completely open ourselves up, and when the other person takes that vulnerability that we have shared and destroys our trust, that person is telling us that we are not worthy enough to stay loyal or respectful to, that our willingness to be vulnerable meant nothing, and that the painstaking effort we took to force ourselves to relinquish control of the carefully constructed lives we have spent our entire lives building for ourselves meant absolutely nothing.

Learning to forgive after a partner cheats, physically or emotionally, is an extremely difficult task that almost no one can fully achieve.

Learning to forgive someone who betrayed and hurt us is a selfless skill that requires extreme amounts of patience, gratitude, empathy, and self-love.

Chapter Thirty-Two

Learning To Love

"Loving others is not the challenge. Loving ourselves is." 𝓛

To be patient is to truly understand that not everyone walks at the same pace.

Some of us are further ahead in our emotional discoveries and experiences when it comes to the kinds of love we seek. Some of us are slower to fall in love and should not be forced or feel obligated to rush into it. Some of us are slower to heal from past experiences and need more time than others before throwing ourselves into something new.

To be patient is to love selflessly when we are not getting what we need from the people we want it from.

To be grateful is to accept the things that we are given, whether big or small.

To be grateful is not to expect lavish grand gestures, but to expect nothing and relish in every small gesture or gift that we are given.

To be grateful is to love our partners for who they are rather than what they can offer us.

Too often, we choose our significant others based on what they have, what they can offer, how they can make us look better in front of our friends and family, and the potential life success that we can have with them. We forget that love comes from what we SHARE with our partners and the lives we can BUILD with them outside of materialism and success.

For just a moment, can we close our eyes and imagine how happy we can be when all we are surrounded by is stuff, stuff that we force our partners to buy for us, so much to the point where we are just collecting, with nothing having value?

Can we truly be happy living inside a mall?

Crazy & Obsessed
Addicted to Relationships

Can we truly be happy when we willingly give people we are supposed to "love" ultimatums?

Can we force someone to buy our love?

Love stems from the willingness to do things for others; love cannot be bought nor can it be bullied into a corner.

Can we picture a life where the only things that exist are us and our partners, two people side by side who are not distracted by anyone or anything else?

Can we live with ourselves then?

Will we still stay with our partners?

Can we truly be happy and in love with the people we are with without any other distractions?

If we cannot, if we cannot picture our lives without our Tiffany jewelry or endless cruises and vacations, then we are in the wrong state of mind. Our minds are only ready for true love when we can honestly say to ourselves that we are completely willing to sacrifice everything for this other person, for this one person who used to be a stranger to us.

Only when we can truly give to ourselves, which can only be achieved through complete self-love and self-acceptance,

Only when we have 100% accepted the selves that we are,

Crazy & Obsessed
Addicted to Relationships

Only when we have absolutely no regrets about our own lives and personal beings,

Only when we have experienced how to love life on our own,

Only when we can give to others without any expectations in return,

Can we truly be in love.

Love is all about giving. Love cannot exist when both parties take nor can love exist when one side gives while the other side takes. When both parties take, we are left with selfish and Machiavellian love, "loving" only to deceive others into giving us what we want. We only enter relationships to take, relationships that will never flourish and eventually drain all parties.

When both sides are constantly scheming against each other to see who can get the most out of the other, both sides lose. When we have relationships in which one side only gives while the other side only takes, we run into scenarios where one side becomes abused while the other becomes too controlling.

The giver is deceived into thinking that he/she is loved because of his/her selfless acts while the taker is constantly scheming to take as much from the giver as possible, getting away with it, and continuing until he/she has fully drained the giver of all life and savings before moving onto the next victim.

Relationships only work when both sides are givers, mutually giving without expectations, and unconventionally expressing love. We cannot rush others, just like we would not like others rushing us, but because we so often neglect the present moment and the other persons, we find ourselves bouncing from one person to the next, unsure of how to love because we are too focused on the future and on ourselves.

To be empathetic is to understand how our partners feel as a result of our actions.

Empathy means being true to the self as well as allowing others to be true to themselves. We are all our own individual persons, and every one of us has the right to love, hate, accept, reject, understand, stay ignorant, and strive for selflessness or greed.

When we are empathetic, we tell those beside us that their lives are just as important as ours, that we are equals, that whatever pains them also pains us, that our troubles and our desires are no better than theirs, that we are not more important, and best of all, that we truly understand rather than just pretend to.

When we show empathy, we show that we care.

But can we be empathetic toward ourselves?

Think about it. We spend so much of our time either focused on taking for ourselves or giving to others that we rarely spend the time to really understand ourselves. Why do some of us only look out for ourselves while others expend more energy looking out for others? Is it necessarily bad that we choose our own wants and our own needs over those of our partners?

Crazy & Obsessed
Addicted to Relationships

On the flip side, can it be bad if we become too involved in pleasing and giving to our partners while neglecting our own needs? Are we giving to our partners because we want to? Or are we only doing so out of insecurity and the fear that they will leave us? Too much time is wasted on whether people want to be with us or just fake it, whether people actually love us when they say it, whether we will get hurt if we continue/change the actions we are currently doing, and whether we should even waste time on unstable love.

Do I love him or do I just love the idea of being in love?

Do I want to be in a relationship or is it because this is all I know?

Is this how my life is supposed to turn out?

Am I so afraid of being alone or the idea of being alone, so afraid of being a social outcast if I am alone, that I force myself to love, blinded to the truth of I really want?

Can I just be alone?

Am I allowed to be alone?

These constant doubts continue to drive us into situations that we may not exactly want. We deceive ourselves into thinking and behaving in certain ways because we have been trained to do so. As children, we never got the chance to discover and understand ourselves before being taught to discover and understand life and humanity, while also being told that only materialism and social interactions can make us happy. We have been told that the ones who live alone are the ones who have been rejected and unloved, people we should not strive to turn into.

But what if these are the people who have discovered the secret to happiness?

The secret to rejecting social standards by understanding themselves fully?

Rather than striving to be with the best or striving to hold onto someone because we believe they "bring out the best in us," we need to strive to, once and for all, understand who we are rather than who we are meant to be. Humans are extremely complex beings where each one of our brains is wired differently, making us special and unique, yet we try too hard to be like everyone else.

We become ashamed of making mistakes because we believe that the more errors we make, the more we steer away from the norm. We run away from ourselves rather than learn to understand how we function, and we let our potential go to waste. We allow others to put us down because they feel threatened by our abilities to shine.

Notice that those who make it (i.e., influencers, motivational speakers, and those who seem to defy the laws of nature) have all rejected the notion that we must live by certain standards. They were the ones who have been hated and exiled for their unconventional beliefs, yet decades later, have managed to change the way we hope to find love and happiness. It is only after others have risked their dignities in attempts to change the world, do we find the strength in ourselves to do so.

Crazy & Obsessed
Addicted to Relationships

It is time for us to stop being followers and start being leaders. We need to learn to take back what we were born to say and how we were meant to live. Humans were not meant to live in silence and fear. Humans were not meant to be overrun by those who are supposedly our equals. Influencers throughout history have made differences, proving that we are capable of speaking from our hearts and still remain supported.

We will always have to deal with haters who criticized how we live, what we say, what we do, how we respond, and even how we feel. But these people are just opinions, opinions that can either be followed or ignored. We can choose to walk away from toxic people whose only purpose is to bring us down. We can choose to walk away from harmful words of others, but we can never walk away from ourselves.

We can heal from others tearing us apart, but extreme guilt arises from self-hate and self-destruction. We are terrified of speaking out against popular opinions, not because it makes others hate us and cast us aside as unwanted and different, but because we are afraid to live with the shame that comes from within ourselves if we do so.

When we speak our minds and opinions in social settings and the majority of the group either rejects our ideas or completely disregards our voices, what do we instantly feel before anybody even gets a chance to criticize or mock us for our "unconventional" opinions (if they even do that)? We immediately feel embarrassed, ashamed, and like we should have never spoken out in the first place.

Crazy & Obsessed
Addicted to Relationships

This is because we are our own worst enemies. We hold ourselves to such high standards that when we have not met them EXACTLY, we beat ourselves up. We tend to believe that the lower the self-esteem someone has and the lower the standards they hold themselves to, the more they hate themselves when things go awry. But it is actually the opposite. When people have low standards of themselves, nothing they do, normal or abnormal, will make them think less of themselves and feel more ashamed of themselves because their self-esteem are already so low.

But, when people have high self-esteem and think highly of themselves, any mistake will make them regret saying or doing ANYTHING at all because they "should have known better." In our minds, whenever we say something we believe is dumb, everyone around us just stops what they are doing and takes their own time and energy to judge us and laugh at us.

In reality, when we say something we believe is dumb, hardly anyone notices, and those who do notice DO NOT CARE. People are socially intelligent enough to know that everyone makes mistakes and everyone has flaws.

People DO NOT CARE if we say the wrong words, trips, slurs, or if we have toilet paper stuck on our shoes (well, they may speak up on the last one out of human decency because toilet paper stuck on our shoes is EMBARASSING!). People just want to go about their days and focus on their own issues and dumb mistakes. We think everyone around us lives in relation to us, that everyone is somehow part of our lives, but they are not. Only a select number of people come into and leave our lives for a reason; the majority of people only coexist with us, completely satisfied never having to interact with us.

But our minds refuse to let us think that way. We are wired to believe that everyone is tied to each other, and one person's mistake affects the thoughts of everyone within a two-mile radius. Our mistakes are our own, and we are the only ones who can truly tell ourselves whether we have made a mistake. When others judge us for making errors, they are simply ignorant to how life works.

We are all focused intrinsically on ourselves, yet we believe everyone is also focused on us, a paradigm that many of us find difficult to break out of.

Chapter Thirty-Three

Be Real

"Place your right hand over the left side of your chest. Do you feel that beating? That is you. That beating is unique to you and not anyone else. Do not let that uniqueness go to waste." ℒ

Humans are the most complicated animals to walk this Earth.

Crazy & Obsessed
Addicted to Relationships

We have the natural instincts of other animals, yet we also have the logic to drive ourselves insane.

We have what it takes to live a simple and happy life, yet we strive to reach toward the unthinkable, setting ourselves up for abysmal failure just so we can relish in high praises and success.

We have the ability to foresee future consequences based on patterns that we have already endured and stored into memory, yet we pursue the same paths over and over, hoping for different outcomes.

We have the resources we need to love and be happy with what we already have, yet we constantly search for reasons to be miserable and reasons to call ourselves "failure."

We do these things because we want to impress those who pay little to no attention to us, to boast what we have to those who do not care, and to hide what we do not have from everyone who breathes. We spend millions and millions of dollars dressing ourselves and our surroundings so we can show off just how insecure we really are when we believe THAT SAME ACT shows off how successful and secure we are. We spend hours and hours editing our lives on social media so we can pretend to have the life that everyone wants.

We go through great lengths to achieve what we believe everyone else wants, not limited to putting ourselves in debt just to chase the dreams that society has constructed for us to follow and/or completely faking how our lives really are through obsessive Photoshopping, to the point where we begin to live in our own lies and neglect who we are outside of others. We were born with minds that can be constructed into anything we want rather than just what we were told. We forget who we are because we try so hard to be those we are not just to impress our egos.

Day in and day out, we only take the steps in life necessary to show ourselves off rather than use that time to improve ourselves. We only do enough to get by rather than what we should to get through life. We want to be seen as "great," but we do not want to take the time and effort to achieve greatness because the illusion is all we need to deceive others. We do not see goals as worth achieving unless we have an audience.

For example, an artist creates a magnificent piece of art, posts it on social media, and receives three likes. Only a select few would continue painting while the rest would give up.

Why?

Because most of us only engage in activities so we can be accepted and well-liked by others rather than activities we actually enjoy. When we do something, such as paint a picture, and the crowd does not go crazy for it as we had expected, we give up because we no longer see a point in doing an activity that no one pays compliments to. That is why those who are able to continue painting after many times of painful rejection are those who paint solely for the love of the art, not for the love of the attention.

Those are the people who live and love for themselves even after failing.

Crazy & Obsessed
Addicted to Relationships

Those are the people who do not need instant gratification and constant attention to continue engaging in activities that they relish in.

Those are the people who are truly living.

Those are the people we should follow.

Depression, self-hate, and low self-esteem all arise from trying to achieve goals we know we can never meet. This is partially due to the impossible standards that society has forced us to meet, resulting in "influencers" Photoshopping their lives in attempts to fool and keep up with the modern world.

We see these falsified images and resent our own lives for not being as "glamorous" as the ones we see online, even when we know that the images we see are not real. We fall into traps of telling ourselves that we are not worthy enough and not good enough because we do not match up to those who have millions of "followers." We hate ourselves and strive to do more, only to fail at attempts of instant gratification and give up, returning to self-loathing and illusions of failure.

What we do not see from influencers obtaining thousands and thousands of likes by the hour are,

Whether these activities are actually from REAL PEOPLE and,

Whether the smiles BEHIND THE SCREENS match the ones on the screens.

Crazy & Obsessed
Addicted to Relationships

We fail to see that most of the world are in the same positions as us, achieving satisfaction and content rather than grandeur and success. We are forced to question whether we are truly happy when we are told that we can be happier if we have much more. We are forced to ignore and doubt the parts of our lives that we once found joy in and conform to parts of others' lives that we deceive ourselves into wanting.

What the hell!?

Why do we find it so easy to give up the things we once loved to chase after things we do not, while at the same time, falling into deep depression and self-hate as a result? Why do we find it so easy to be influenced by things we are smart enough to know are not true? We are intelligent creatures, with minds that can extend beyond unimaginable beliefs. We can GIVE endless advice on how we should not be falling for these schemes but struggle when it comes to taking our own advices.

We are intelligent at reasoning and working through problems but struggle tremendously when it comes to overcoming the mental blocks that prevent us from being able to stand our grounds and hold onto our desires and beliefs. Known as being one of the most difficult tasks that any human being will ever endure, self-love is a daunting one that many of us have attempted but few have achieved.

Complete self-love means giving ourselves undeniable and unconditional love despite all external factors that sway us otherwise.

Crazy & Obsessed
Addicted to Relationships

Complete self-love means waking up every morning and going to bed every night without the need to compare ourselves to those we assume have it better.

Complete self-love is fully accepting ourselves for all the flaws we have even when others are telling us that we should not.

There are endless courses, lectures, self-help books, and "Psychology Today" articles that target our vulnerable sides when we do encounter brief moments of poor self-esteem, and we fall for their gimmicks. First, these sellers are only playing the game by knowing the EXACT moments we need "help" and when we will succumb to their false advertisements. Second, there is NOTHING wrong with us! We only fall for these marketing schemes and believe that this placebo effect works because we doubt our own mental strengths to survive without the help from "professionals." We were taught that we must strive to improve and be the "best," insinuating that there is something wrong with us.

How often do parents tell their children that they are perfect as they are rather than telling them they must change and improve in order to make it successfully and fit in with the rest of the world?

This is not necessarily the parents' fault, however. We live in a society where we are FORCED to change in order to SURVIVE. We blame parents too often for "not accepting their children," but really, most parents are only trying to build our strengths to make it in a world where they struggled to. That is why it is extremely difficult for us to snap ourselves out of feeling like we must reject who we should be and strive for who we are.

But, remember, the human mind can endure feats of greatness, including accomplishing even the most difficult of tasks.

Take a moment.

Close your eyes.

Imagine.

Bring yourself into the place where you are most happy.

What do you see?

Are you struggling to create an answer that you feel is acceptable and not completely stupid?

Well, stop it.

You do not need to come up with one.

The fact that you could even PICTURE a place means you can achieve self-fulfilling happiness and can change the mindset that you were taught to follow. Most of us still struggle with creativity because we associate it with rebellion, which in turn, becomes associated with going against the "correct" standards of life.

When we are stressed, angry, or frustrated, we often like to go on long drives or close our eyes and imagine that we are in a happier place, aka our safe zone. We have all the skills we will ever need to live the lives we want, but we still feel the need to rely on others because we were told to. Some people spend years in relationships and

Crazy & Obsessed
Addicted to Relationships

friendships that are toxic to them but feel obligated to stay for show.

We still believe that if we are not in a committed relationship by a certain age then there must be something wrong with us.

I once dated someone who seemed really confused that I was still single, immediately assumed that there was something "wrong" with me, and refused to take "nothing" as an answer. We look at people's outside appearances and automatically assume whether they are single or taken. We still associated "beautiful" people with being in relationships and "ugly" people with being single forever.

We still associate being single with being unwanted, so when we are chased, our egos become so enlarged that we believe we are entitled to it.

We are creatures of dichotomous thinking. When we have nothing, we believe we do not deserve anything. When we receive something, we believe we deserve it all. These, again, are lies that we have been fed. We are not selfish in nature, but the fables and fairytales we have been told since birth turn us into selfish beings.

I want to walk out my front door, without a man by my side, without a ring, without a short haircut, without a giant wart on my face, without my arm hanging off my body, and without acting like I am facing the apocalypse, and just walk down the street, undisturbed.

Crazy & Obsessed
Addicted to Relationships

I do not need unwanted men coming up to me and thinking they are entitled to a date just because I am not married.

I do not need a man escorting me across the street because I learned how to cross the fucking street when I was two.

I do not need people asking me over and over why I am single just because I am.

I want to be able to travel alone to foreign cities without seeming like I want to sell myself.

I want to flirt on first dates without people assuming I am reaching for sex.

I want to JUST BE NICE to another human being without SOMEONE thinking that I am either flirting, home-wrecking, or prostituting.

I want to look in the mirror one day and tell myself that it is completely okay just being me.

Just me.

I want us to all join together, to make a pact to each other and to ourselves, that we will at least TRY (because I know that promises almost always fall through) to ACKNOWLEDGE that these crazy relationships and dating problems we have are results of our transient and fleeting emotions, and that they DO NOT REFLECT who we are as people.

The next time we freak out over someone who breaks up with us out of nowhere and decide to aimlessly Facebook stalk him/her for weeks, REMEMBER that this does not make us stalkers. This makes us caring intellectuals who have shared our hearts and have had them broken. This makes us mature adults who had some wrong turns in life.

This makes us beautiful hearts who were not given the same love we had dealt. If caring too much and feeling hurt as a result of not receiving care back from people we had openly trusted makes us crazy, then fine, we are FUCKING CRAZY then.

Just because we become emotional from pain does not mean we should be locked up.

Just because we spew out crazy and insane statements about how much pain we are in does not make us at risk to ourselves.

Just because we handle betrayal by drinking, stalking, and hooking up with strangers rather than cry one tear, do yoga, and wake up automatically feeling better, which, by the way, NEVER HAPPENS because NO ONE walks away from a breakup, long or short, scar-free, does not mean we are "handling a breakup wrong."

Even those who cheat and crave to be with people other than their partners feel pain when it comes to a breakup.

Despite how difficult the relationship was, despite how much two people should not have been with each other, and despite how much two people find extreme happiness in others, there was a time and place where two separated individuals felt a connection to each other, felt joy, and felt the love that gravitated them toward each other in the first place, so much that, even if the breakup was justified or mutual, there will always be that sense of betrayal and the feeling of "what if."

From the outside perspective, or even when we have had some time to recover from our own traumatic experiences, the end of a relationship happens every day, and all the clichés that usually occur in relationship advice come into play. Even the best relationship therapists all narrow down their sessions to one take-home message: It will all be okay.

Will it, though?

Physically, yes.

As time moves on, humans see issues that were once amplified as no longer as serious as time helps to forget and distract, not necessarily heal. Even if we feel less congested mentally, and we are no longer in tears all the time, does that really mean we are "better"? Does that really mean we are "healed"? Even though we are no longer actively hyper-focused on a situation, it does not mean that we are not still affected by it.

In my personal experiences, this is the breakdown of my emotions over the course and end of a relationship:

Deeply in love and willing to do anything to keep this person happy.

Telling myself I am going to marry this person.

Hating this person and everything about him.

Crazy & Obsessed
Addicted to Relationships

Hating myself for hating this person and unsure of whether to leave or stay, even after endless arguments and abuse.

Stalking and obsessively trying to contact this person after the relationship ends.

Stalking and obsessively trying to contact this person's family after the relationship ends.

Crying nonstop for months every time something reminds me of this person.

Trying to distract myself from this person by drinking heavily and dating every single person who expresses interest in me.

Completely ignoring my values and my sense of self by sleeping with strangers.

Ending at rock-bottom after waking up next to someone I do not recognize.

Coming to my senses by replacing men with activities that I could do alone.

Forgetting why I was so obsessed over this one person and no longer wanting to be with him or contact him.

Finding happiness in my life again and no longer wanting it to end.

Constant thoughts of the craziness and insanity that I am capable of...?

Crazy & Obsessed
Addicted to Relationships

Number 14 is something that many of us either do not realize or ignore because we feel physically fine otherwise. We are no longer a mess, and we are no longer actively thinking about our exes. But that lingering feeling of what we are CAPABLE OF DOING, or that feeling of when a demon is taking over our bodies, never really goes away.

We may be healed physically, but after each experience of "craziness" that we go through, our self-esteem goes down, our anxiety and trust levels go up, and we never really recover from the creeping memories of who we can become when we are in pain. This prevents us from wanting to start new relationships, we become extra clingy to try to prevent our new partners from ending it with us, or we go with the classic "I will break up with you before you can break up with me." We do not see it as serious problems now, and some of us do not even realize that these feelings are manifesting until we are already deep in them. No one, not even the best therapists, can unravel how our behaviors affect us subconsciously.

Our patterns continue because we never fully address the past. We focus on the present moments, trying to heal from the pain we feel CURRENTLY. We do not think about the future consequences of not dealing with these feelings before getting into new relationships until AFTER the patterns repeat.

We let ourselves become scarred by the people we are capable of becoming, and because we never address them, we are left with this lingering feeling that something is wrong with us.

I am not normal.

Crazy & Obsessed
Addicted to Relationships

I will admit it.

I am addicted to love.

I fall in love too quickly.

I drive myself and others up the wall when I feel that love is fading away.

I experience losing a relationship the same way I experience being stabbed in the chest by a sharp knife.

I risk my life and dignity just so someone will stay with me.

I willingly allow others to walk over me and take advantage of me because I fear they will leave otherwise.

I tell myself and the person I am with that I am in love with him too soon into the dating phase, and I have trouble separating love from infatuation and loneliness.

I go back to exes and people I used to know when my dating life seems catastrophic, and I move too fast and then wonder why I am unlovable.

I give others what they need right off the bat, and I leave myself, and my heart, with nothing.

I stalk exes and obsessively contact their family in hopes for second chances when I have done nothing wrong and even when I am no longer in love.

I crave attachment and the idea of knowing I am with someone rather than wanting to be with someone.

Crazy & Obsessed
Addicted to Relationships

I threaten to hurt myself and make up fake aliases to give exes reasons to not ignore me and keep them around for as long as possible.

I refuse to let people go even when I am with someone new, and I become overwhelmed with rage when they are no longer interested in me.

I disclose my entire life to complete strangers in hopes that the pity card wins me brownie points.

I am addicted to love.

And I am okay with that.

Epilogue

The Turn Around

Three years later...

The phone rings

Me (picks up): Hello?

Him (enthusiastically): Hey! It's me!

Me (fully knowing who is on the other line): Who's "me"?

Crazy & Obsessed
Addicted to Relationships

Him (confused): It's me! J! Remember?

Me (still fully knowing): No...I really don't...

Him (still confused and slightly disappointed): You really don't remember me?! Are you serious? We dated for almost seven years!

Me (aloof and annoyed): Oh, right. Hi.

Him (excited): Hi! How are you!??! It's been awhile!

Me: Yeah.

Him: Hey! I was wondering if you want to grab a drink and catch up!

Me: I don't think so.

Him: Come on! One drink! As friends! It'll be fun!

Me: Yeah, I still don't think so.

Him (in a serious tone): Alright, the reason I called is because I've been thinking about us a lot, and I think I'm ready to get back together, you know, give this thing another shot and see how we do.

Me (thinking): Who the fuck does this kid think he is?! Three years to think!?? What, two years of partying, half a year of hooking up, another half of drinking, and a day of thinking? Cool. Cool. I feel so much better! THANK YOU SO MUCH FOR THINKING OF ME!

Crazy & Obsessed
Addicted to Relationships

Me (irritated): This thing? Is that what our relationship meant to you? Just a thing?

Him (defensive): That's not what I meant. I'm just trying to tell you that I want to try again.

Me: Why?

Him: Because I think I still love you, and I know you still love me so, what do you say? Let's get back together! I forgive you, and I'm ready to try again!

Me: No.

Him: No? What do you mean? I do forgive you. Let's go out to dinner tomorrow!

Me: No.

Him (persisting): Come on! We can even split the bill! You don't even have to pay for me this time!

Me: No.

Him: No? What do you mean "no"?

Me: I mean no.

Him: But didn't you hear me? I still love you. I thought this was good news because you still love me.

Me: I don't love you anymore.

Him (confused): You don't love me?

Crazy & Obsessed
Addicted to Relationships

Me: Oh my god. Get it through your thick narcissistic head. I DO NOT LOVE YOU ANYMORE! I DO NOT WANT TO GET BACK TOGETHER! I NEED YOU TO LEAVE ME ALONE!

Him: Wait, how do you not want to be with me? You're in love with me, and I'm giving you another chance. Are you seeing someone else? You're cheating on me?!

Me: Dude, regardless of whether I am seeing someone or not, which is none of your fucking business, I can't cheat on you because WE ARE NOT TOGETHER.

Him: But you're my girl. We promised to love each other no matter what.

Me: That promise was destroyed when you broke up with me three years ago.

Him: But I'm here now, and I want you back. You're mine forever. I love you.

Me: Dude, no! I don't belong to you! I don't love you. In fact, I still very much HATE YOU. NOW LEAVE ME ALONE!

Slams the phone down

Him (via text): Why'd you hang up on me!? I still love you, and I want to be with you.

Silence

Him (via text): Please talk to me. I know you're there!

Crazy & Obsessed
Addicted to Relationships

Silence

Phone rings

Voicemail

Phone rings

Voicemail

Him (via text): Please pick up the phone! Stop ignoring me! I love you!

Silence

Phone rings

Voicemail

Phone rings

Voicemail

Phone rings

Blocked

Two days later, outside my apartment...

Him (cheerfully): Hey! What a coincidence running into you here! I was just in the neighborhood! I completely forgot that you live here! There was something wrong with my phone, and we must have lost connection the night I tried to call you. So, this is perfect! We can talk in person!

Crazy & Obsessed
Addicted to Relationships

Me: Dude, are you fucking stalking me?

Him (dumbfounded): What? Of course not! I was just grocery shopping in the area, turned the corner, and there you were!

Me: You live in Jersey. You drove an hour and a half to come out here to grocery shop?

Him: I like the stores here better.

Me: The only store near here is Wholefoods, and you have one ten minutes from you. Plus, you're not even carrying grocery bags!

Him: I didn't see anything I like.

Me (scoffs): You're impossible.

Starts walking away

Him: Wait! Can we talk?

Me: There's nothing to talk about.

Him: I want to talk about us.

Me: There is no us.

Him: Lena! Please!

Me: We are done. For good. Bye.

Him: LENA! DON'T WALK AWAY FROM ME! DO YOU KNOW WHO I AM?! I KNOW YOU STILL LOVE

ME! WE CAN MAKE IT WORK! PLEASE! COME BACK!! I LOVE YOU!! I CAN'T LIVE WITHOUT YOU!

Continues walking away

Him: I DON'T WANT TO LOVE ANYONE ELSE BESIDES YOU!! I LOVE YOU SO MUCH! PLEASE TALK TO ME!!

Silence

Gone

Silence

The wind blows softly against the barren trees of autumn, whistling tunes of the forgotten, leaves fleeting across the roads.

Him (whispering): I love you....

Conclusion

We Are Over. Right?

"Sometimes we need to simply let go, let go of control, let go of promises, let go of hope, let go of the "what ifs." Then, maybe, we can begin to recover." 𝒧

Part of me knew my ex was going to come running back. They always do. They only want us when we no longer want them, turning into the obsessive lovers that we once were. Do I regret walking away from him when all I wanted, for months, was him? Does part of me wish I had said yes to his request of getting back together? Probably, but at that moment, my brain was strong enough to overtake my heart.

That IMPULSIVE DECISION to turn him down saved me from a life of toxic love, otherwise, I would not be writing this book right now. Do I still think about him from time to time? We all do; we just hate to admit it. We all have some regrets when it comes to who we are with, who we have been with, where we are, and who we are. We will always have struggles with relationships, and we will always have memories of past struggles with relationships.

Maybe one day we will get back together.

Maybe not.

That decision is not up to me.

That decision is in the hands of life.

All I can say is, at the moment, I do not want him in my life.

But, then again, what do I know?

Will it ever get easier dealing with uncertainty and anxiety of potential heartbreak before, during, and after a relationship?

I wish I could stay positive and give you something to look forward to about love, but the short and cold answer is: no. Unlike many aspects in life, love is something that cannot be controlled, and the more we realize that there is nothing we can do about who love us and who do not,

Crazy & Obsessed
Addicted to Relationships

the more we want to try to control it. We want what we cannot have, and it drives us insane. With relationships always come uncertainties, and some of us would rather stay single than deal with the rollercoaster of emotions that comes with being with someone else.

After ten mind-fucked years of dealing with:

Flakey men

Broken promises

Suicide attempts

Criminal-like behaviors

Back and forth never-ending relationships

Lack of trust

Intense hatred for myself and others

Anger for the behaviors people are capable of, and

Complete self-destruction,

I still find myself in a mind-fucked situation.

It does not matter who I am with, how great the person I am with is, or how great I currently feel about my life and situation, the anxiety and constant paranoia will always be there. I am constantly overthinking every step I make in a new relationship, and how much I do not want to fuck up again because I know the events I am capable of spiraling down into if it does get fucked up.

Crazy & Obsessed
Addicted to Relationships

I keep telling myself that if a new relationship ends, changes are going to be made on my end, I will get my shit together and act like an adult, and I will keep my emotions under control. But that does not ever happen, and that will not ever happen, because I cannot predict how my emotions will respond to certain situations. Who knows, I can very well wake up one day, lose the love of my life, and be completely content.

Sometimes I wonder why I let the loss of love affect me so much, even when I know I use it to replace something lacking in my own life. Sometimes I wonder how my love life would have been like if I had not let my emotions catalyze my self-destructive and catastrophic behaviors. Would I still be with one of my exes because my crazy behaviors would not have pushed them away? Or would I still be in the same position I am right now, realizing, with a clear head, that on-and-off relationships almost never work out?

Do I regret a lot of decisions I had made?

Of course.

Would I change how I react to breakups if I could go back in time and do so?

Probably not.

Because if I did, I would be acknowledging that who I am is flawed and needs to be "fixed." I would be acknowledging that feeling pain and having emotions are sins. I would be acknowledging that I need to become a completely different person in order to fit in with this world.

Crazy & Obsessed
Addicted to Relationships

That is never going to happen.

Stay strong.

Let the crazy within you flourish.

I Love You

Crazy & Obsessed
Addicted to Relationships

Crazy & Obsessed
Addicted to Relationships

Crazy & Obsessed
Addicted to Relationships

www.ingramcontent.com/pod-product-compliance
Lightning Source LLC
Chambersburg PA
CBHW020401080526
44584CB00014B/1123